940.53 AYL

The Era of the Second World War

J F AYLETT

THE LIBRARY
WYCLIFFE COLLEGE,
STONEHOUSE,
GLOUCESTERSHIRE.

The era of the Second World War

102510

Non-Fiction   940.53 AYL

Wycliffe College

ACC NO: 1552

Hodder & Stoughton
LONDON SYDNEY AUCKLAND

ACKNOWLEDGEMENTS

The Publishers would like to thank the following for permission to reproduce illustrations in this volume: Popperfoto-cover; Jean-Louis Charmet Collection p5; David King Collection p6 left; The Communist Party Picture Library p6 right; The British Museum p7 both; The Weimar Archive p8 left; The Communist Party Picture Library p8 right; Popperfoto p9 left; The Hulton-Deutsch Collection Ltd p9 right; United Nations Library, Geneva p10; Punch Publications p11 top, p11 lower left; The British Library p11 lower right; Topham Picture Source p12; By permission of the Development Team for the Suntory Museum Project, Osaka p13; Moro Roma p14; The Hulton-Deutsch Collection Ltd p15 left; Moro Roma p15 right; The Weimar Archive p16 left; Topham Picture Source p16 right; Bundesarchiv, Koblenz p17 left; The Communist Party Picture Library p17 right; The Hulton-Deutsch Collection p18; Archiv Für Kunst und Geschichte, Berlin/© DACS 1993 p19 left; David Low, Solo Syndication and Literary Agency/John Frost Historical Newspaper Service p19 right; Moro Roma p20 both; The British Library p21 left; Associated Press p21 right; T & V Holt Associated p22 left; The Weimar Archive p22 right; The Hulton-Deutsch Collection Ltd p23 right; The Communist Party Picture Library p24; The Bibliothèque Nationale p25 top; The Imperial War Museum p25 lower; Courtesy of the Library of Congress p26 left; David King Collection p26 right; Clifford Berryman, Washington Star/Courtesy of the Library of Congress p27 left; Süddeutscher Verlag p27 right; Robert Hunt Library p29; T & V Holt Associates p30; The Imperial War Museum p31 top left; T & V Holt Associates p31 lower left; Popperfoto p32 left; John Frost Historical Newspaper Service p33 left; T & V Holt Associates p33 right; Turner Entertainment Inc./British Film Institute, Stills, Posters & Designs p34 left; Robert Opie Collection p34 right; The Imperial War Museum p35 left; T & V Holt Associates p35 right; Bildarchiv Preussicher Kulturbesitz p36 left; The Imperial War Museum p36 right; Bildarchiv Preussicher Kulturbesitz p37; Topham Picture Source p38, p39 left; Royal Air Force Museum p39 right; Ullstein Bilderdienst p40; Novosti Press Agency p41 left; Bildarchiv Preussicher Kulturbesitz p41 right; E.T. Archive p42 left; Honolulu Advertiser p43 top; The Imperial War Museum p43 lower; John Laver p45 left; Novosti Press Agency p45 right; The London Cigarette Card Company p46 left; T & V Holt Associates p46 right; The Hulton-Deutsch Collection Ltd p47 left; Popperfoto p47 right; From the former 'Desiderata' Collection, as reproduced in 'I'll Be Seeing You', T & V Holt Associates p48 left; The Imperial War Museum p48 right; Robert Hunt Library p49 right; The Weimar Archive p50; Rex Features p51; Bildarchiv Preussicher Kulturbesitz p52; The Imperial War Museum p53 left; Topham Picture Source p53 right; Bildarchiv Preussicher Kulturbesitz p54 left, p54 lower right; Popperfoto p54 top right; © Robert Capa/Magnum p55; Bildarchiv Preussicher Kulturbesitz p56 left; The Weimar Archive p56 right, p57; U.S. National Archives p58, p59 left; Robert Hunt Picture Library p59 right, p60 main picture; The Hulton-Deutsch Collection Ltd p60 inset; Akiko Takakura p61; Photri p62; Bildarchiv Preussicher Kulturbesitz p63 left; M Hooks p64; Topham Picture Source p65 left; The Imperial War Museum p65 right; Popperfoto p67 left; The Imperial War Museum p68; David Seymour/Magnum p70 left; The Weimar Archive p70 right, p71 left; The Hulton-Deutsch Collection Ltd p71 right; T & V Holt Associates p74 right; The Hulton-Deutsch Collection Ltd p75 top; Popperfoto p75 lower; Coca-Cola Great Britain & Ireland p76 left; Warner Bros/British Film Institute Stills, Posters & Designs p76 right; Popperfoto p78 left; The Hulton-Deutsch Collection Ltd p78 right; Robin Mackness p79 top.

The Publishers would also like to thank the following for permission to reproduce copyright material in this volume: *Daily Express* for the extract from *Daily Express*, 31 May 1940; *Daily Mirror* for the extract from *Daily Mirror*, 4 September 1939; Hamish Hamilton Ltd for the extracts from *Mischling, Second Degree* by Ilse Koehn, copyright © 1977. Published in Great Britain by Hamish Hamilton Ltd, 1978; Longman Group UK for the extract from *The Modern World Since 1870*, L E Snellgrove, 1968 and the extract from *Hitler and Germany*, B J Elliot, 1966; Times Newspapers Ltd for the extracts from *The Sunday Times*, Garth Alexander (1.12.91) and Sam Kiley (13.5.90), © Times Newspapers Ltd, 1990/91.

Every effort has been made to trace and acknowledge ownership of copyright. The Publishers will be glad to make suitable arrangements with any copyright holders whom it has not been possible to contact.

Orders: please contact Bookpoint Ltd, 39 Milton Park, Abingdon, Oxon OX14 4TD. Telephone: (44) 01235 400414, Fax: (44) 01235 400454. Lines are open from 9.00 – 6.00, Monday to Saturday, with a 24 hour message answering service. Email address: orders@bookpoint.co.uk

Illustrations by Philip Page

British Library Cataloguing in Publication Data

Aylett, J. F.
 Era of the Second World War. – (Past Historic Series)
 I. Title II. Series
 940.53

 ISBN 0 340 58362 2

First published 1993
Impression number   11 10 9 8 7 6 5 4 3 2
Year   2004 2003 2002 2001 2000 1999 1998

© 1993 JF Aylett

All rights reserved. No part of this publication may be reproduced or transmitted in any form or by any means, electronic or mechanical, including photocopy, recording, or any information storage and retrieval system, without permission in writing from the publisher or under licence from the Copyright Licensing Agency Limited. Further details of such licences (for reprographic reproduction) may be obtained from the Copyright Licensing Agency Limited, of 90 Tottenham Court Road, London W1P 9HE.

Typeset by Litho Link Ltd, Welshpool, Powys, Wales
Printed in Hong Kong for Hodder & Stoughton Educational, a division of Hodder Headline Plc, 338 Euston Road, London NW1 3BH by Colorcraft Ltd.

CONTENTS

'If you know your own history, you have a good start for the future'

       – the Mayor of East Berlin (1990).

THE LEGACY OF THE GREAT WAR

The Great War ended in November 1918. The winners spent the next few months drawing up a peace treaty. The main decisions were made by the leaders of three countries – the United States, Britain and France. The Germans had lost and were not invited.

Woodrow Wilson, the American president, knew what he wanted. He wished to make a peace settlement which would last; he wanted to avoid another war.

The French leader, Clemenceau, also wanted to avoid another war but he set about it in a different way. He wanted to punish Germany for starting the war and make it pay for the damage which had been done. A weak Germany could not start another war.

Lloyd George, the British Prime Minister, knew that many British people felt much the same. But he was worried. He believed that a harsh treaty might have the opposite effect: the Germans might be so bitter that they would want revenge.

A peace treaty with Germany was signed at Versailles on 28 June 1919. Coloured foam bubbled from the fountains in the palace gardens to celebrate the official end of the war. But not everyone was happy. Germans were already meeting to protest in the city of Berlin.

In fact, the Versailles Treaty was just the first of a series of agreements. In 1919, separate treaties were made with Austria-Hungary and Bulgaria; in 1920, it was Turkey's turn. The map of Europe had been redrawn.

Woodrow Wilson believed that each nationality should have its own country. In fact, this was just not possible. The new country of Yugoslavia contained various different nationalities. And over three million Germans found they now lived in Czechoslovakia. Each was to cause problems in the future.

B What happened to Austria-Hungary.

Millions of men had fought in the Great War; three of them were to be important in the years to come. One of them was an Austrian who had fought in the German army. He had been a brave soldier, twice awarded the Iron Cross. His name was Adolf Hitler.

A These were the main terms of the Versailles Treaty.

E David Evans: *Europe in Modern Times* (1981).
The statesmen who met in 1919 to redraw the map of Europe faced a near impossible task. In solving one problem, they created others; in satisfying one country, they disappointed another. Historians have criticised the treaties and blamed the politicians for virtually all the disasters which [happened to] Europe afterwards.

F Edgar Mowrer: *Germany Puts the Clock Back* (1933).
Could a better treaty have been made in the atmosphere of hatred [and] vengeance [at] the Paris Peace Conference? I think it could have been made by wiser, braver men.

Only 40 per cent of French men aged between 20 and 32 in 1914 were still alive and well in 1918.

C This French cartoon showed the Allies redrawing the map of Europe.

Hitler was bitter that the war had ended. He thought that the politicians had let down the German army. He was also angry at the Versailles Treaty. In future years, he would promise 'to tear it up'.

Benito Mussolini, an Italian, was another bitter ex-soldier. Italy gained land as a result of the treaties – but not as much as it hoped to get. Mussolini felt that Italy had been badly treated at the peace talks.

But a third ex-soldier called Winston Churchill had learned a different lesson from the war. He believed that the war showed that Britain must maintain its military strength. He thought this was the only way to stop other countries from becoming aggressive.

Each of these men would play a decisive part in the years to follow. So, too, would the leaders of Russia which had also fought in the war. What had happened to *them* would be equally important for the world over the next 20 years.

D This clause of the Treaty of Versailles blamed Germany for the war.
. . . Germany accepts the responsibility of Germany and her allies for causing all the loss and damage to which the [Allies] have been subjected as a result of the war.

1 Write down the nationality of each of these people:
(a) Woodrow Wilson; (b) Lloyd George;
(c) Clemenceau; (d) Churchill; (e) Mussolini;
(f) Hitler.
2 a) Read sources E and F. How do they disagree?
b) Suggest a possible reason why they disagree.
3 a) Look at sources A, C and D. Write down as many reasons as you can why Germany would feel bitter.
b) Write down any other reasons you can find in this chapter.
c) Which do you think was the most important reason? Explain how you decided.
4 a) Look at source A. What evidence is there that the allies wanted to punish Germany?
b) Please give a detailed answer. Did the allies want to punish Germany and, if so, why?

COMMUNISM

A Marx: a Russian banner of 1933.

The Great War had one other major effect. The German, Austrian and Russian empires were split up. The Russian Emperor himself was murdered in July 1918. More important, Russia had been taken over by communists.

Communism was an idea which had been invented by a German writer called Karl Marx. In 1848, he explained his ideas in a book called *The Communist Manifesto*.

The world, he wrote, was divided into three classes of people. The rich had capital (money) so he called them capitalists. They used this money to build factories. When the factories made a profit, the capitalists grew even richer. They were supported by a middle class of people, including shopkeepers and office workers.

Everyone else belonged to the working class. Marx called them the proletariat. These people worked in the factories for long hours but earned little money. The capitalists were their enemy.

In 1848, this was a fair description of many factories. The owners *were* rich – and some workers *did* hate them. But Marx did not just describe life at the time. He also predicted what would happen in the future.

The time would come, he said, when the workers would not put up with this for any longer. They would revolt. Capitalists and workers would fight – and the workers would win.

After this revolution, the peasants would share out the land; the workers would run the factories. Everyone would have a share of the profits. There would be no rich people: everyone would be equal. This new system was 'communism'.

Marx did not think the workers could cope with this all at once. At first, the workers' leaders would have to make the decisions and get things organised. But, in time, the workers would do all these things for themselves.

These ideas appealed to many Russians. One of them was a Bolshevik, known as Lenin. In November 1917, he organised the workers' revolution which Marx had written about. Within two months, the Bolsheviks had taken over power and Russia became a communist country. It was one of the major events of the 20th century: its effects would be felt far beyond Russia.

B This 1920 magazine tried to persuade workers everywhere to become communist.

Прежде

Один с сошкой, семеро с ложкой.

Теперь

Кто не работает, тот не ест.

ВРАГИ ПЯ

ПОМЕЩИК СМОТРИТ ЗЛЫМ БАРБОСОМ,　ШИПИТ ПРОДАЖНЫЙ ЖУРНАЛИ
КУЛАК СОПИТ БУГРИСТЫМ НОСОМ,　ОСТРИТ КЛЫКИ КАПИТАЛИСТ,
ПЬЯНЧУГА С ГОРЯ ПЬЕТ ЗАПОЕМ,　МЕНЬШЕВИЧОК ВО-ВСЮ ЯРИТСЯ,
ПОП ОГОЛТЕЛЫМ ВОЕТ ВОЕМ,　ВОЯКА БЕЛЫЙ МАТЕРИТСЯ,—

C This Russian poster showed scenes before and after the revolution. The caption to the top picture (before the revolution) reads: 'One to work, seven to eat'. The lower caption says, 'He who is not working does not eat.'

Posters are often produced as propaganda. In other words, they aim to spread ideas and get people to believe them. Historians can learn a great deal from sources like this. For instance, they show what some people believed at the time. They may also show the methods used by politicians to persuade people to support them.

D From *The Communist Manifesto* by Karl Marx (1848).
Let the ruling classes tremble at a Communist revolution. The proletarians have nothing to lose but their chains. They have a world to win.
WORKING MEN OF ALL COUNTRIES, UNITE!

E This Russian poster from the 1920s shows some of the enemies of communism. They are a rich peasant, a drunk, a priest and a landlord who is always away from his farm.

1 a) In your own words, explain what Marx said would happen.
b) Whom did he say would benefit?
c) Whom did he say would lose?

2 a) Who is the person in source B?
b) What exactly is he doing?

3 a) Study source E and read the caption. Which person is which?
b) Why do you think communists thought each was a threat? Give a different reason for each person.

4 Which of the pictures do you think are propaganda? Explain how you made your choice.

5 Which source is best for understanding why rich people were afraid of the communists? Give reasons for your choice.

6 a) How reliable are sources B, C and E? Explain carefully.
b) Even if they're not reliable, can we learn anything from them? Please answer in detail.

WEIMAR GERMANY

On 9 November 1918, the German Emperor escaped to Holland. He left behind a country in a state of revolution. Armed gangs roamed the streets. Getting back to normal was not going to be easy.

In January 1919, a new Assembly was elected. It met in the little town of Weimar; the town gave its name to the new republic – Weimar Germany.

The new government had no shortage of problems. It had to sign the Versailles Peace Treaty, ending the war. The agreement was harsher than the Germans had expected. The government unfairly got the blame.

On top of this, the Germans were forced to pay for the damage they had done during the war. In 1921, the amount was fixed at £6600 millions. The German economy was already in a bad state. Having to pay reparations only made matters worse.

Reparations were partly paid in goods – coal and wood. In December 1922 some wood for France did not arrive. So the French decided to take matters into their own hands. In January 1923, French and Belgian troops moved into the Ruhr industrial area.

A The communists were active in Weimar Germany. This was one of their posters.

B This anti-communist poster was produced by the Bavarian People's Party. It reads: 'The Bolshevik is loose!'

The Germans fought back. The Ruhr workers went on strike and the German government supported them. The bitterness was understandable; the results were a disaster for the German economy. The value of the German mark fell rapidly.

Germany was already suffering from inflation. In 1919, a British pound was worth 250 German marks; by August 1921, there were 760 marks to the pound. A year later, there were 35,000 marks to the pound. During 1923, inflation got completely out of control.

By summer, wages were paid daily. The workers spent them at once while they were still worth something. People who ordered a drink in a cafe paid for it when it arrived. If they left it until later, the price might have gone up. It was even worse for retired people: pensions became worthless overnight. Some people gave up the struggle and committed suicide.

A new German government sorted out the inflation problem in 1924. But the years 1919-23 had a lasting result. Many people had joined one of the small political groups which had grown up. One of them was the National Socialist German Workers' Party – or Nazi Party. Its leader was Adolf Hitler.

RED for socialism

WHITE for nationalism

BLACK was the symbol of the struggle for Aryan man's victory.

C The swastika became the symbol of the Nazi Party in 1920. The flag came into use in the same year. The captions explain what it stood for.

Who decided to use the swastika?

D *Hitler and Germany* by B J Elliott (1966).
The first step was to design an emblem, a party flag, and here [Hitler] could use his artistic talent. After many attempts he produced a black crooked cross, in a white circle upon a red background. [It was] an ancient symbol known as the swastika.

E *Making History* by Christopher Culpin (1984).
After the war, [Hitler] went into politics. He showed himself to be a brilliant speaker and organiser. The swastika and the rallies were his ideas.

F *Hitler* by Joachim Fest (1974). *Mein Kampf* was a book written by Adolf Hitler in 1924.
In *Mein Kampf* Hitler pretended that the swastika flag was his invention. In fact, one of the party members, the dentist Friedrich Krohn, had designed it for [a] local party group in May of 1920.

G Hitler with some supporters in 1923. They included Emil Maurice, who was Jewish. In later years, the Nazis attacked the Jews, so Maurice was blacked out. Look for his boots, to the left of Hitler.

Secondary sources may disagree for all sorts of reasons. For instance, there may be a shortage of primary sources – or a primary source may be unreliable. As a result, it is sometimes possible to find a secondary source which is wrong.

1 Write down *all* the effects of these events:
a) the treaty of Versailles;
b) the payment of reparations;
c) French troops marching into the Ruhr.

2 a) Look at source B. What is the communist about to do?
b) How does the poster help to stir up hatred for communists?

3 a) Read sources D, E and F. How do sources E and F disagree?
b) What opinion is contained in source E? Explain how you know it's an opinion.
c) Can sources E and F both be correct? Explain your answer.
d) What two interpretations of the origin of the swastika can you get from these sources?
e) Describe the strengths and weaknesses of each account.
f) Why would Hitler have wanted people to believe that he invented the swastika symbol?

4 'Source G has been changed so it's not a reliable source.' Do you agree? Please explain your views in detail.

THE LEAGUE OF NATIONS

Two ways in which the League of Nations could stop countries fighting. The League did not have an army of its own.

There was one other lasting effect of the war. The American President Woodrow Wilson wanted to set up an international organisation which would stop another war. In 1919, it came about. They called it the League of Nations.

In fact, the League had two jobs. The first was to keep peace in the world; the second was to make the world a better place to live in by encouraging countries to co-operate.

Countries which joined the League signed an agreement called the Covenant. They promised not to go to war to gain land. And they promised to help any country that was attacked. If a war did start, the League could punish the country which attacked. The pictures above show how it could do this.

This all sounded very reasonable. But, first, countries had to join the League. If a lot of countries didn't, then sanctions could not work. There would still be plenty of countries willing to trade with the attacking country.

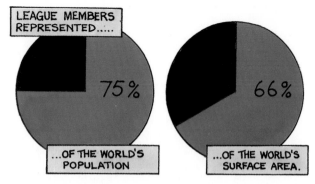

A Membership of the League grew from 27 nations in 1919 to 60 in 1934.

This was the first thing that went wrong. When the League was set up in 1919, several major countries did not join. Germany was not allowed to join until 1926 and the USSR did not join until 1934 – the same year in which Germany left. But the biggest blow was when the United States itself refused to become a member.

Despite this, the League had some early successes. It settled a dispute between Finland and Sweden; in 1925, it actually stopped a war between Greece and Bulgaria.

However, its weaknesses soon became obvious. In 1931, Japan invaded Manchuria. The following year, the League ordered Japanese troops to leave Manchuria but they did not. Instead, Japan left the League of Nations. No sanctions were ever imposed.

Other countries learned the lesson: the League had very little power. They, too, would ignore the League over the next few years. In 1937, the building of the League's headquarters in Geneva was finally finished. By then, it hardly mattered. The League was a dead duck – and war was only two years away.

B The League helped over 2 million refugees to get home and find work. This passport was issued to them.

Cartoonists' views of the League

The League was a favourite subject in cartoons of the 1920s and 1930s. These are three British ones.

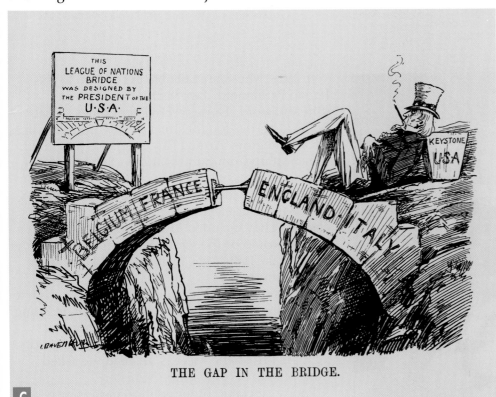

THIS LEAGUE OF NATIONS BRIDGE WAS DESIGNED BY THE PRESIDENT OF THE U·S·A·

KEYSTONE USA

BELGIUM FRANCE

ENGLAND ITALY

THE GAP IN THE BRIDGE.

C

Cartoons do not show real situations. If they did, they would not be funny. In source C, the cartoonist is not suggesting that US President Woodrow Wilson really sat beside a bridge and smoked a cigar. The cartoon is a joke based on what actually happened. Cartoons are nearly always biased but that does not stop us learning a great deal from them.

OVERWEIGHTED.

President Wilson. "HERE'S YOUR OLIVE BRANCH. NOW GET BUSY."
Dove of Peace. "OF COURSE I WANT TO PLEASE EVERYBODY; BUT ISN'T THIS A BIT THICK?"

D

E This cartoon appeared in 1936 after Italy had conquered the African country of Abyssinia (Ethiopia).

1 a) Read page 10. What reasons are given to explain why the League was a failure?
   b) Which of these do you think was most important? Give reasons.

2 a) Study source C. What does the bridge represent?
   b) Why is the middle piece missing?
   c) What point is the cartoonist making?

3 a) Study source E. What does the baby represent?
   b) Who are the men and why are they running away from the baby?

   c) What point is the cartoonist making?

4 Study source D. Does the cartoonist think the League will work? Explain how you decided.

5 a) Please answer in detail. How do these cartoons help us understand public attitudes towards the League of Nations?
   b) Which one best helps to explain why the League was a failure? Explain your answer.

2

MUSSOLINI AND ITALY

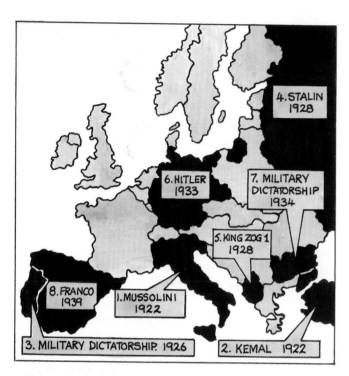

A Dictators gained control in many countries between the wars.

In 1915, Italy had joined the allies against Germany in the Great War; about 600,000 Italians were killed or wounded. As a result, Italians hoped to gain land from the peace treaties. But Italy gained little and the people felt let down by the USA, Britain and France. Italians felt much bitterness.

Peace did not make life better. Taxes had gone up to pay for the war. Now, there was unemployment and inflation. Even a loaf of bread cost five times what it had in 1915. Yet wages had risen less than prices. Factory workers showed their anger in riots and strikes.

Governments came and went; none of them seemed able to deal with the country's problems. In this situation, many people looked for extreme solutions. The very poor thought communism might be the answer and they hoped for a revolution.

Others were just as determined to stop a communist revolution. One of them was a journalist called Benito Mussolini. In 1919, he started his own political party, called the Fascists. His followers included unemployed ex-soldiers. The rich, too, supported him: they did not want the country to be taken over by Communists.

In 1919, Mussolini failed to get elected to the Italian Parliament. Two years later, it was a different story. These were violent times. Rival political parties fought street battles, armed with sticks and guns. Armed Fascist squads joined in: they beat up Communists and Socialists in street brawls.

About 200 people were killed in the months before the 1921 elections – and 36 Fascists were elected. They included Mussolini. He told Italians that he would be the strong leader they needed: he could make Italy great again; he could deal with the Communists.

In October 1922, Mussolini felt strong enough to bid for power. The Fascists would march on Rome and take over the government. The army was brought out to stop them but the king would not let them fire on the Fascists. Instead, he asked Mussolini to become Prime Minister.

Four years later, other political parties were banned: only the Fascists remained. Parliament stopped making laws: only Mussolini had the power to do so. He had become a dictator – the first of many in Europe.

B Mussolini. People called him Il Duce (you pronounce it doo-chay). It means 'the leader'.

1919-Bolscevismo-   *1923-Fascismo-*

C This Italian poster showed the contrast between life under Communists (on the left) and life under Fascists (on the right).

Did life improve under the Fascists?

D An American writer, Howard Marraro, described life under the Fascists in *Current History* magazine (1935).

The Italian today is much better fed than he was. The standards of living of the Italian people have improved from 1913 to the present. This improvement is [greatest] during the twelve years of Fascist [rule].

Thanks to Fascist [laws], there has been no important strike in Italy since 1926.

The economic and social achievements of Fascism are impressive . . . a more prosperous and happy nation.

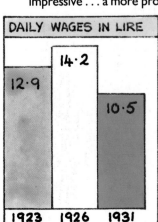

DAILY WAGES IN LIRE

12·9	14·2	10·5
1923	1926	1931

REAL WAGES (i.e. WHAT THE WAGES WOULD BUY)

107	89	87
1923	1926	1931

E Wages of Italian farm workers (from the *International Labour Review*, 1932).

F George Seldes: *Sawdust Caesar* (1936).

It is true that there has not been one first-class strike since 1926. In every instance where workmen threatened or began a strike the Fascist militia has [stopped] it with violence and bloodshed. The Labour Charter [bans] strikes. The militia see that the charter is enforced.

G Mussolini told Parliament in 1930:

Fortunately, the Italian people are not used to eating several times a day. As they have a modest standard of living, they feel suffering less.

---

1 Put these events in the order they happened and put the date beside each:
   a) The march on Rome;
   b) Mussolini started the Fascist Party;
   c) Mussolini elected to Parliament;
   d) Mussolini became Prime Minister.

2 Why did Mussolini come to power? (There is more than one reason.)

3 a) Study source C. What impression does it give of life under the Communists?
   b) What impression does it give of life under the Fascists?
   c) Which political group do you think produced this poster? Explain how you decided.

4 a) Study sources D and F. Which one contains more opinions? Give reasons.
   b) Do you think source D is correct? Give reasons.
   c) What two interpretations of life in Fascist Italy do you get from the sources? Please answer in detail.

ITALY ATTACKS ABYSSINIA

Italian weapons included flame-throwers and mustard gas. Italy had signed an international agreement not to use poison gas; Mussolini said they hadn't used it.

The League of Nations imposed sanctions on Italy but other countries went on trading with her; in any case, oil was not on the banned list. Even Mussolini admitted that a ban on oil would have caused the Italian attack to fail.

In May 1936, Italian troops entered the Abyssinian capital. The King of Italy gained a new title: Emperor of Abyssinia. Mussolini told the people, 'The Italian people has created the empire with its blood.' But it was mainly Abyssinian blood. There were just 5000 Italian casualties but nearly 500,000 Abyssinians had died.

However, the war was expensive. Throughout Italy, women had handed in their wedding rings to help pay for it. Even so, a year's money had been spent on winning a country with few resources. More important, there was no chance of Britain and France ever siding with Italy again.

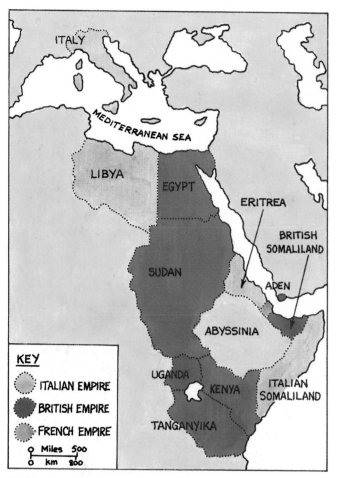

A Colonies in Africa in the 1920s.

Mussolini wanted Italians to be proud of their country. He reminded them of the great days of Ancient Rome, when Romans controlled much of Europe. In the 1920s, even the Mediterranean Sea around Italy was controlled by the British, not by the Italians.

Mussolini was jealous of the British and their empire. He wanted Italy to have a bigger empire of her own. It would make other countries respect her more. But most lands were already part of someone's empire. There were few lands left for him to conquer.

One of them was Abyssinia in North Africa. It was a poor and backward country but it was an ideal target – right between Eritrea and Italian Somaliland. Italy already owned them both.

Mussolini had long been telling Italians that war was good. In 1935, he set about proving it.

Half a million Italians were sent to conquer Abyssinia. It was the biggest army ever to fight in Africa. The war which followed was a very one-sided affair. The Abyssinians fought back but their weapons were mostly out-of-date.

B This Italian painting showed Italian soldiers freeing Abyssinian slaves.

C An Abyssinian soldier killed in the war.

Did France and Britain support Mussolini?

D Countess Edda Ciano was Mussolini's daughter. She described a visit to London in an interview in 1989.

I met MacDonald, who was the [British] Prime Minister at the time. I insisted on knowing if the English would go to war against Italy.

He said, 'No.'

Then I added, 'But will you take any action?'

'Yes, of course, but we won't make war.'

'That's settled,' I replied. I don't know if we shook hands. I can't remember.

E Graves and Hodge: *The Long Week-end* (1941).

The question was: how far would the sanctions policy be carried if the Italians did invade Abyssinia? There was a [belief] in French and British Government circles that it would be a [good] thing to let the Italians have a try at Abyssinia. If they succeeded, they would be kept busy for years trying to colonize that hopeless country; if they failed, they would be weaker still.

F Rosaria Quartararo, an Italian author, gave this account in 1989.

Before beginning his expansion into Abyssinia, Mussolini asked Britain and France for their permission. The French gave their consent in January 1935. The English remained [not clear] for months.

G Giampiero Carocci: *Italian Fascism* (1972).

The British government wished to avoid war at all costs because of the weakness of the British navy. This weakness made such a war seem completely out of the question.

H An Italian newspaper printed this drawing of Italian troops in action.

1 Give as many reasons as you can in your answers.
   a) Why did Mussolini want to increase his empire?
   b) Why did he choose to attack Abyssinia?
   c) Why did he deny using poison gas?

2 a) Look at sources B and C. What different ideas do they give of the war?
   b) Look at source H. How reliable do you think this picture is? Please answer carefully.

3 a) Please read page 14. Write down all the causes of Italy's victory over Abyssinia.
   b) Please read all the sources. Write down any other causes you can find.
   c) Which do you think was the most important cause? Give reasons.

4 'Britain helped Italy to conquer Abyssinia.' Do you agree with this statement? Please write a detailed answer, showing how the causes were linked.

HITLER COMES TO POWER

In 1923, the year after Mussolini's march on Rome, Hitler decided to copy the idea. He organised a march on Berlin. Unlike Mussolini, it did not bring him power; instead, it got him a jail sentence.

In prison, he wrote a book about his ideas. It was called *Mein Kampf* – 'My Struggle'. However, it would be some years before he could put these ideas into practice. The German economy improved between 1924 and 1929. There was little support for Hitler's policies.

By 1930, it was a different story. A slump in the United States meant that German businesses had to do without American loans. Many went bankrupt; people lost their jobs. Hitler saw his chance.

He promised to find work for the unemployed. He said he would ignore the Treaty of Versailles: no more reparations. There would be no more Communists either: he would crush them. He also promised to deal with the Jews. He claimed they were causing all Germany's problems.

In the 1932 election, the Nazis became the biggest single party in the Reichstag. In January 1933, Hitler became Chancellor of Germany. In March 1933, fresh elections were held; again, the Nazis were the largest party.

B Hitler receives flowers; a photograph taken before 1936.

Soon afterwards, Hitler got the Reichstag to pass an Enabling Law. It gave him the right to make laws without asking Parliament. Hitler now had all the power he needed. He quickly set about using it.

By the end of 1933, trade unions had disappeared. Their place was taken by an organisation called the 'Labour Front'; it was run by the Nazis. And all the other political parties were banned. Only the Nazis remained.

Even Boy Scouts were banned; by 1936, boys were forced to join the Hitler Youth Movement instead. Schoolchildren were soon using new textbooks; they were written by Nazis. Books the Nazis did not like were banned – and burned. Hitler wanted to make sure that Germans thought only what he wanted them to think.

At first, these changes only affected Germany. But Hitler had other policies, too. He wanted all Germans to live inside Germany. In other words, he intended to take over other countries.

A A poster from the 1932 election: 'German women, think of your children. Vote Hitler.'

Why did people support Hitler?

C Egon Hanfstaengel described Hitler's early speeches.

[They] consist [mostly] of ravings and rantings against the Treaty of Versailles. I am prepared to say that without the Treaty of Versailles – no Hitler.

D Dr Philipp Jenninger, speaking in 1989.

A man wrote to me: 'I was unemployed for many years. I would have made a pact with the devil, if I had been given work. Then Hitler came along and I got work, so I followed him.'

E This is from a British textbook: *Making History* (1984).

The new Nazi Party soon began to attract attention. This was partly because the programme offered something for everyone, but it was also because of the violence of [Hitler's] supporters. Hitler had set up an armed force within the Party: the Stormtroopers or SA. They were directed to keep order at Party meetings. Later they broke up the meetings of opponents and stopped them from speaking.

G This Czech cartoon of 1933 was called 'Popular Enthusiasm'.

H In 1989, Henry Metelmann recalled how it felt to be a member of the Hitler Youth.

It was a great feeling. You felt you belonged to something great. You felt you belonged to a great nation which now finds its feet again. Germany now was in good safe hands and I was going to help and build a strong Germany. Lovely feeling.

It is not possible to discover why people supported Hitler by studying just one source. This page contains just a few sources which offer reasons. If you think carefully, you will find that each picture offers at least one extra reason. Remember, too, to be on the look-out for propaganda.

Ganz Deutschland hört den Führer mit dem Volksempfänger

F This Nazi poster says 'All Germany listens to the　Führer　'. The Nazis put on sale one of the cheapest wireless sets in Europe – and controlled broadcasts.

1 What was each of the following: (a) Mein Kampf; (b) the Reichstag; (c) the Enabling Law and (d) the Labour Front?

2 a) What changes took place in Germany from 1933 onwards?
b) Which of these changes were political ones?
c) Which of these changes were social ones?
d) Did these changes bring progress? Please answer carefully.

3 a) Read the written sources. What different reasons do they give for why people supported Hitler?
b) How useful are the pictures for understanding why people supported Hitler? Please answer carefully.
c) Which source is most useful for understanding why people supported Hitler? Give reasons for your choice.

4 a) Pick any one of the pictures that you think is unreliable as evidence. Explain how you chose it.
b) Look again at your choice. Write down, in detail, what we can learn from it.

HITLER'S FOREIGN POLICY

A Europe in 1936. German troops marched into the Rhineland.

Hitler had told the German people that he would ignore the Treaty of Versailles. The Allies knew that there was little they could do about it. They could not stop Germany from making more weapons. Nor could they stop Hitler increasing his army.

In 1935, Hitler announced that military service would become compulsory for men. He wanted an army of 500,000. He also said that Germany would rearm. Each was forbidden in the Treaty of Versailles.

The Treaty also stopped Germany having troops within 50 km of the River Rhine. It was a demilitarised zone. The idea was to keep German troops away from France.

In March 1936, German troops marched back into the Rhineland. No one stopped them. Only Poland looked like taking action, but no one supported them. Indeed, some British politicians thought Hitler had every right to be there.

But the Rhineland had been a test to see if Britain and France would act. Hitler now knew the answer. This was important because Hitler had plans which went far beyond the Rhineland.

Hitler believed that Germans were the master race; everyone else was inferior. So he wanted all Germans to be living on German soil. But Hitler believed that Germany did not have enough farmland to feed all these people.

So he also wanted *lebensraum*. It means 'living space'. In his search for this land, Hitler looked east. There was land in Poland and Russia – and he wanted it.

However, attacking Poland would have been risky. The French might have launched a surprise attack. Then, the Germans would have to fight on two fronts – just as in the Great War. Putting troops back in the Rhineland solved that problem. A surprise French attack was now impossible.

Hitler still felt that Germany would be safer if it had an ally. He would have liked an alliance with both Britain and Italy. But, in 1935, Mussolini had attacked Abyssinia and Britain had opposed this. So Hitler had to choose: he chose Mussolini. In 1936, the two made an agreement, known as the Rome-Berlin Axis.

B Hitler and Mussolini in Munich in 1938. Luftwaffe chief Goering is seen on the left.

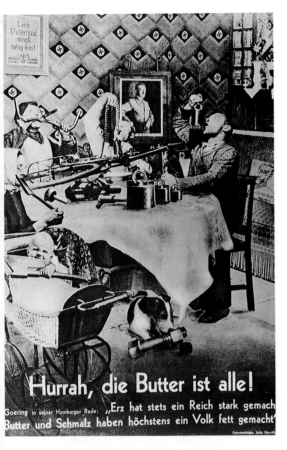

Lieb
Vaterland
magst
ruhig sein!

Hurrah, die Butter ist alle!

Goering in seiner Hamburger Rede: „Erz hat stets ein Reich stark gemach
Butter und Schmalz haben höchstens ein Volk fett gemacht"

Fotomontage: John Heartfield

C 'Hurray, the butter is all gone!' This 1935 German picture mocks German rearmament. Goering's quote below reads: 'Empires have always grown strong on iron ore; butter and lard have, at best, made a nation fat!'

D Hitler's interpreter, Paul Schmidt, described events in 1936 in *Opera Mundi* (1951).
More than once, even during the war, I heard Hitler say: 'The 48 hours after the march into the Rhineland were the most nerve-racking of my life.' He always added: 'If the French had then marched into the Rhineland, we would have had to withdraw with our tails between our legs.'

E Ivor Matanle explained why Britain did nothing in *The Hitler Years* (1984).
In Britain, Baldwin [the Prime Minister] said that British public opinion felt that Germany had done little more than [free] her own territory. The government could not act against such opinion.

F Harold Nicolson gave an extra reason why Britain did not act. From his *Diaries and Letters, 1930-39* (published 1966).
We know that Hitler gambled. If we send an ultimatum to Germany she ought to climb down. Naturally, we shall win and enter Berlin. But what is the good of that? It would mean communism in Germany and France. Moreover, the people of this country refuse to have a war. We should be faced by a general strike if we even suggested such a thing.

G William Shirer, an American journalist, wrote his views in *Berlin Diary* (published 1941).
BERLIN, March 8.
Hitler has got away with it! France is not marching. Instead it is appealing to the League! No wonder the faces of Hitler and Goering were all smiles this noon at the State Opera.

Oh, the stupidity (or is it the paralysis?) of the French! I learned to-day that the German troops which marched into the Rhineland yesterday had strict orders to beat a hasty retreat if the French army opposed them in any way. They were not prepared or equipped to fight a regular army.

LATER. – I called our London office to see what the British are going to do. They laughed, and read me a few extracts from the Sunday press. The *Observer* and the *Sunday Dispatch* are *delighted* at Hitler's move. The British are busy restraining the French!

"HOW MUCH WILL YOU GIVE ME NOT TO KICK YOUR PANTS FOR, SAY, TWENTY-FIVE YEARS!"

H A British cartoon of 1936 showed Hitler facing western politicians.

---

1 Why did Hitler want (a) a bigger army, (b) *lebensraum* and (c) German troops in the Rhineland?

2 a) Draw the map on page 18. Colour in (i) Germany, (ii) the Rhineland and (iii) Italy.
   b) Which country or countries would feel most frightened after the Rome-Berlin Axis? Explain how you decided.

3 a) How do sources E and F disagree about why Britain did not act?
   b) What is William Shirer's view (in source G)?
   c) Do you think the cartoonist (source H) would have agreed with source G or not? Give reasons.

4 a) Which sources support the view that Britain was wise not to act? Explain your choices.
   b) Which sources support the view that Britain was foolish not to act? Explain your choices.

1920	1930	1940	1950	1960	1970

The Rome-Berlin Axis had its first test in 1936 when civil war broke out in Spain. The Republican government had taken land away from the Catholic Church and rich landowners. These changes caused violent opposition.

In June alone, 61 people were assassinated. The following month, a group of Spanish army officers in Morocco decided to act. They took control of three Moroccan towns and shot government officials.

One of these officers was called General Franco. He returned to Spain to lead the rebellion against the Republicans. Most of the army was on his side; so was the Church and the *Falange*, the Spanish Fascist Party.

They were opposed by the Socialists and Communists, who included most trade union members. Each side killed its opponents: Franco's Nationalist supporters shot trade unionists while the Republicans killed Catholic priests.

Britain and France refused to get involved. Even the League of Nations told other countries not to interfere. But Hitler and Mussolini paid no attention.

B This Italian postcard promises that Italian Fascists will destroy Spanish Communists.

The war gave Hitler the chance to test German aeroplanes and their young pilots; they tried out dive bombing techniques and tested how accurate their equipment was. Mussolini, too, sent guns and aeroplanes, along with up to 70,000 troops.

The USSR supported the Republicans with weapons and advisers. But they did not get anything like the help that Hitler gave the Nationalists. It was inevitable that, in the end, Franco would win.

The world saw the war as a fight between Fascists and Communists. In fact, it was more of a local dispute. In March 1939, the capital, Madrid, was captured by the Fascists. Franco had won. Europe could add another dictator to its list of rulers.

Hitler and Mussolini hoped that Franco might become an ally. But Spain stayed neutral in the Second World War. Franco used the time to build his country. He also hung on to power: he remained dictator of Spain until his death in 1975.

A This poster showed one side's opponents in the war. Franco's slogan ('Spain Arise') is shown on the mast.

Who destroyed Guernica?

The town of Guernica was captured by Nationalists during the war. On 26 April 1937, it was almost destroyed. Who did it – the Republicans, the Nationalists or the Germans?

It is quite common to find two very different accounts of an event. Every source has weaknesses and strengths. The historian has to weigh up each source and decide who is telling the truth.

BRITAIN, FRANCE, SCANDINAVIA, THE UNITED STATES, ALL THE CIVILISED WORLD HEARD WITH HORROR YESTERDAY OF THE BOMBING OF MEN, WOMEN AND CHILDREN IN GUERNICA, ANCIENT CAPITAL OF THE LOYAL BASQUES.

German airmen, fighting for rebel General Franco and flying German bombing 'planes, swept down from a clear sky on the defenceless, peaceful town. They left it, three hours later, a town of death and fire, its little white houses ablaze, the narrow cobbled streets paved with dead and dying.

At least 800 people were killed; several thousands were wounded.

Fugitives were pursued into the fields by the airmen and shot down as they ran.

C This was the report in a British newspaper of 28 April 1937. The headline read: 'German Airmen Atrocity Shocks World'.

D This was a Nationalist press release of the time.

Guernica was destroyed by incendiaries and petrol, was bombed and converted into ruins by the [Communists].

E Peter Kemp fought on Franco's side in the war. This was what he later wrote.

I learned [the truth] from two journalist friends who entered the town on 29 April. The Nationalist – not the German – air force did bomb Guernica. The burning and destruction of the town were the work of Republicans.

F The Mayor of Guernica gave his version in a speech in May 1937.

It was not [Republicans] who set fire to Guernica. I swear before God and history that German aeroplanes bombed viciously and cruelly our beloved town until they had wiped it from the earth.

G Father Alberto de Onaindia claimed to be an eye-witness. He later recalled:

An aeroplane appeared over Guernica [followed by] a squadron of seven planes followed a little later by six more, [then] by five more. All of them were Junkers (German planes). For more than an hour these eighteen planes dropped bomb after bomb on Guernica. Bombs fell by thousands.

The aeroplanes left around seven o'clock. Then there came another wave dropping incendiary bombs. [It] lasted thirty-five minutes. I realised the terrible purpose of this new act of vandalism. They were dropping incendiary bombs to try to convince the world that the [people] fired their own city.

H Guernica after the bombing.

---

1 a) Look at source A. Who do the three numbered people represent?
   b) Look carefully. What are these people doing to Spain?
   c) Which side do you think produced the poster? Explain how you decided.
   d) This poster is propaganda. Even so, what can we learn from it?

2 Study this page thoroughly.
   a) What different interpretations of the event are given?
   b) Write down which interpretation each source supports.
   c) Pick any two sources which you think might not be reliable. Explain why you have doubts about them.

3 Now, write down your own interpretation of what happened at Guernica. Refer to the sources in your answer.

Hitler wanted all Germans to be living inside his new Germany. He himself was Austrian so he was very keen to join Austria to Germany. This was another thing which had been banned in the Treaty of Versailles.

What Hitler wanted was an *Anschluss* (union) of Germany and Austria. The Austrian Chancellor tried to avoid a union. So, in 1938, he arranged for a   plebiscite   . All Austrians would be asked whether they wanted Austria to stay independent.

In March, the day before the vote was due to be held, German soldiers marched into Austria. Austrian troops did not resist: there was no point. Hitler got his Anschluss and this postcard celebrated the event.

13·MÄRZ 1938
EIN VOLK EIN REICH
EIN FÜHRER

A

Within a fortnight, Hitler had a new demand. He wanted the north-western part of Czechoslovakia, called the Sudetenland. There were about 3 million Germans living there. It also contained heavy industry and the main Czech defences.

B Chamberlain arrives to talk to Hitler in September 1938.

In September, the British Prime Minister, Neville Chamberlain, flew to Germany to discuss the Sudetenland with Hitler. Back in Britain, gas masks were issued; people began digging trenches, in case there were air-raids. But no one wanted a war; most Britons hoped that the Czechs would give in.

In all, Chamberlain made three trips to see Hitler. The last meeting was at Munich. The Czechs were present but were not allowed to take part in the talks. Britain and France had already decided that Hitler could have the Sudetenland.

An agreement was signed and, on 1 October 1938, German troops entered the Sudetenland. Hitler said he wanted no more land in Europe. Chamberlain flew back to Britain and waved the agreement for everyone to see. 'I believe,' he said, 'it is peace for our time.'

Bookmakers offered odds of 32-1 against war in France. But the French Prime Minister, Daladier, now thought that war was inevitable. In fact, it was less than a year away.

C Josef Goebbels was Nazi Minister of Propaganda. He made this comment on his job.

Nothing is easier than leading the people on a leash. I just hold up a dazzling campaign poster and they jump through it.

Two Views of the Anschluss

D This is what a German woman wrote in her diary (*Nazi Lady*, published in 1978).

March 12th

We have invaded Austria – the newspapers say that the communists are   pillaging   and shooting in Vienna. Goebbels has spoken on the radio. I am excited, and so is everyone here. The Austrians are welcoming our troops with joy.

E This is what William Shirer, an American journalist, wrote in his diary (*Berlin Diary*, published in 1941).

On an aeroplane: March 12

Vienna was scarcely recognizable this morning. Swastika flags flying from nearly every house. Where did they get them so fast? I bought the morning Berlin newspapers. Amazing! Goebbels at his best, or worst! Hitler's own newspaper on my lap here. Its screaming [headline] across page one: GERMAN-AUSTRIA SAVED FROM CHAOS. And an incredible story describing [communist] disorders in the main streets of Vienna yesterday, fighting, shooting, pillaging. It is a complete *lie*. But how will the German people know it's a lie?

G Hitler listens to a speech by the Sudeten Nazi Party leader (1938).

F Poster celebrating the Anschluss (1938). The caption reads: 'People to people and blood to blood.'

1 What job did each of these people have: (a) Hitler; (b) Chamberlain; (c) Daladier and (d) Goebbels?

2 a) Draw an outline of the map in source A.
   b) Place a cross at two places where you might expect Hitler to want land. Explain your choices.
   c) Look at the map on page 28. In which two countries was this land?

3 Read sources C, D and E.
   a) How do D and E disagree?
   b) Which one do you think is correct? Explain how you decided.
   c) What two versions of the Anschluss can you get from these sources?
   d) How does source C help you to understand source D?
   e) Why would Goebbels want Germans to believe what the newspapers said? Please answer in detail.

APPEASEMENT

GERMANY HAD BEEN HARSHLY TREATED AT VERSAILLES.

TREATY
GERMANY

BRITAIN WAS TOO WEAK TO FIGHT GERMANY.

HITLER WOULD STOP THE COMMUNISTS.

BRITISH FORCES COULD NOT HELP CZECHOSLOVAKIA BECAUSE OF WHERE IT WAS

GERMANY
POLAND
CZECHOSLOVAKIA
AUSTRIA
HUNGARY
ITALY
ROMANIA
YUGOSLAVIA

IT WAS A SACRIFICE WORTH MAKING FOR PEACE.

RIP
CZECHO-
SLOVAKIA

BRITAIN COULD NOT RELY ON THE USSR: IT WAS TOO WEAK AND UNRELIABLE.

COMMUNISM
— KEEP OUT

Why did western leaders do nothing to stop Hitler? There is no one answer. These two pages look at some of the causes of appeasement. It is an important issue. This policy helped to cause the Second World War.

A Some of the arguments put forward in favour of appeasement.

When Hitler took over Austria, western politicians did nothing. When Hitler demanded the Sudetenland, Chamberlain and Daladier gave in. Why?

The reason is that Britain and France followed a policy called *appeasement*. In effect, it meant letting Hitler have what he wanted. Chamberlain hoped that eventually he would be satisfied – and war would be avoided.

Appeasement was a popular policy with most electors. Many people believed that it was only fair for Germany to get back what it had lost in the Versailles Treaty. Few people outside Germany had read *Mein Kampf*. Few politicians realised that there was no limit to Hitler's demand for *lebensraum*.

However, half of the British Cabinet was opposed to appeasement and even Chamberlain did not trust Hitler. As early as 1937, he saw Germany as a possible enemy. He began to re-arm Britain.

B A Russian cartoon of the 1938 Munich agreement. Daladier and Chamberlain direct Hitler towards the USSR (CCCP).

Why appease Hitler?

C Chamberlain wrote to his sister in March 1938.
Nothing that France or we could do could possibly save the Czechs from being overrun by Germans. I have therefore abandoned any idea of giving a guarantee to Czechoslovakia or to the French in connection with that country.

D He also wrote to her:
Is it not horrible to think that the fate of hundreds of millions depends upon one man – and he is half-mad?

E The French General Jean Delmas said in 1989:
In September 1938 the French army was in no state for intervention.

F A French historian said why he thought the French followed a policy of appeasement (1989).
France was in no position to think of war after 1914-18. Her sacrifice had been so great. Pacificism was a gut [feeling] in all parts of society.

G Lord Boothby visited Europe in the summer of 1938. In August, he met Chamberlain. He described what Chamberlain said in *My Yesterday, Your Tomorrow* (1962).
I gather you [think] that the gangster element among the Nazis is now in control, and that they will stick at nothing. I like to stick to things even after there seems no chance of success.

H Robert Graves and Alan Hodge: *The Long Week-end* (1941).
In Britain, Munich at first seemed a victory. Peace had been preserved. Appeasement had triumphed. All was well again. As Chamberlain himself said: 'I have no doubt, looking back, that my visit alone prevented an invasion for which everything was prepared.' 'Thanks to Chamberlain,' wrote Lord Castlerosse, 'thousands of young men will live. I will live.'

I Quintin Hogg described his views in 1938 in *Picture Post* (1970).
A democracy can only go to war united. In September 1938 the nation was deeply divided. The nation was [not] ready to admit that the Second World War was inevitable.

J A J P Taylor: *The Origins of the Second World War* (1961).
At the beginning of 1938, most English people sympathised with German grievances. The Sudeten Germans had a good case.

K (Above): Czech children with German soldiers in the Sudetenland, October 1938.

L (below): Adults give their welcome.

1. a) Look at sources K and L. Do the people welcome the Germans or not? Give reasons.
   b) How reliable are these photographs? Explain your answer.
2. Study the rest of these two pages carefully.
   a) List the causes of the policy of appeasement.
   b) Which of these causes were military?
   c) Pick two causes which you think were most important. Give reasons for your choices.
   d) Source B suggests a different reason from all the other sources. What is it?
   e) Which of the reasons at the top of page 24 seems to support the Russian view? Explain your answer.

THE SOVIET UNION'S ROLE

A German cartoon showing Stalin (1937).

Hitler and Mussolini were just two of the dictators of the 1930s. Another was Joseph Stalin, the leader of the   Soviet Union   . When the leaders met at Munich in 1938, the Czechs weren't the only ones not invited. The Soviet Union was not represented, either.

Western countries did not trust the Russians. Soviet radio broadcast Communist propaganda to the world in 17 different languages. This frightened the capitalist nations; they became very suspicious of the Russians.

The Russians even said they looked forward to another war. They claimed it would help communism to spread. In fact, the Soviet Union was just as scared of war as anyone else. The country was just not ready: it did not have the weapons.

Once Hitler came to power, the Soviet Union was in a very dangerous position. The Nazis hated the Communists. There was a risk they might attack the Soviet Union. So, in 1934, the Soviet Union joined the League of Nations. But Stalin could not get western countries to join him in standing up to Hitler.

Hitler had promised that he wanted no more land after he took over the Sudetenland. Once again, he lied. In March 1939, German troops took over the rest of Czechoslovakia. Once again, Britain and France did nothing.

Stalin did not need a crystal ball to guess that Hitler's next target was Poland – and that would put German troops on the Soviet border. If it came to war, the Germans would win. Stalin was worried that France and Britain might ally with Germany, leaving the Soviet Union to fight alone. So Stalin looked for an ally. It had to be either Germany or Britain.

In the summer of 1939, there were talks between Britain and the Soviet Union. The Russians tried hard to persuade Britain to make an alliance with the Soviet Union. But Britain did not think that the Soviet army could stand up to the Germans.

Stalin did not trust Britain and France, either. After all, they had not stood up to Germany in the past. So he decided to play it safe; he also held talks with the Germans. On 23 August, the world heard the result: Germany and the Soviet Union had signed a pact. When war came, they would not fight each other.

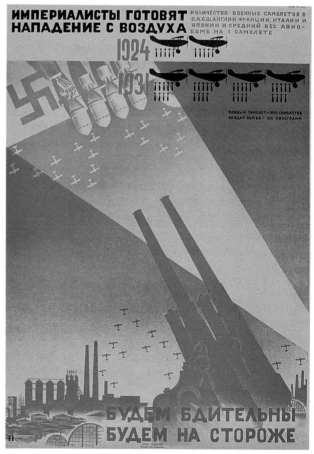

B This Russian poster warns that the Fascists are preparing to attack from the air.

Why did Stalin sign the Pact?

WONDER HOW LONG THE HONEYMOON WILL LAST?

C An American view of the Nazi-Soviet Pact (October 1939).

D A Soviet historian gave his view of the Pact (1979).
The Soviet government did not deceive itself regarding Hitler's aims. It understood that the treaty would not bring the USSR lasting peace but only a breathing-space. The Soviet government [used] the time to strengthen its defence.

E A different Soviet view was given in an American film of 1943. An actor playing the part of Stalin says this.
[Certain people] in England have determined [to make] Germany strong. At the same time, they shout lies about the weakness of the Russian army. There's no doubt that their plan is to force Hitler into a war with this country. Then, when [we] have exhausted ourselves, they will step in and make peace.

F Sir Fitzroy Maclean was a British diplomat in the Soviet Union at the time. He gave his view in 1990.
Hitler offered Stalin what he hoped was peace which he needed very badly to pull the Soviet Union together. We were offering him a front-line position in the nastiest war there'd ever been.

G An American view, from a newsreel commentary of November 1939.
Many believe that Soviet Russia, by remaining neutral, will emerge as the only [winner] in the Second World War. As the rest of Europe exhausts its resources and manpower, they see Soviet Russia growing stronger and stronger.

H Stalin toasts Hitler's health after the agreement is signed (August 1939).

Historians must try to work out why people acted as they did – their motives. Often, these can turn out to be causes of later events.

1 a) Why did Stalin not trust the western countries?
   b) Why did the western countries not trust Stalin?

2 a) What impression of Fascists do you get from source B?
   b) What impression of Stalin do you get from source A?
   c) How do these two sources help to explain why western countries were surprised by the Nazi-Soviet Pact?

3 a) Each written source gives a different reason why Stalin signed the pact. Write them all down.
   b) Write down Stalin's attitude towards Hitler, using all the written sources.
   c) Which source do you think gives the main reason for the pact? Explain your choice.
   d) Why might a historian have doubts about source E?
   e) What can a historian learn from source C?

GERMANY INVADES POLAND

In March 1939, German troops took over the rest of Czechoslovakia. It was still winter when the German army reached Prague, the capital. The Czechs showed their anger by throwing snowballs at the tanks. It was all they could do.

In April, Mussolini invaded Albania. But the world's eyes were turned to Hitler. He now had a new demand. He wanted the Polish corridor, a strip of Polish land which separated one part of Germany from the rest.

KEY:
OCCUPIED BY GERMANY
S ~ SWITZERLAND
H ~ HOLLAND
B ~ BELGIUM
E ~ ESTONIA
L ~ LITHUANIA

Everyone could see that appeasement had failed. In March, Britain and France promised to support Poland if she were attacked. In early April, Hitler gave secret orders for the German forces to be ready to attack Poland on 1 September 1939. In May, Germany and Italy signed an alliance, called 'The Pact of Steel'. Each nation promised to help the other, if it came to war.

But Mussolini was nervous: he thought that a war with Poland would lead to a much wider war. Hitler disagreed. He said, 'I am convinced that neither England nor France will embark upon a general war.'

Meanwhile, Britain was getting ready for war. All men aged 20 and 21 were conscripted in May. The newspapers said it was a good idea – it would make them fitter. The first young men signed on in June.

During August, there were reports of clashes between German and Polish troops on the frontier. On 23 August the Soviet Union signed its agreement with Germany. The Polish government saw what would happen next. The following day, Polish troops were mobilised for war.

What Poland didn't know was that the Nazi-Soviet Pact had a secret clause. Germany and the Soviet Union had agreed to carve up Poland between them. This agreement was not revealed until after the war.

Hitler had already decided to attack Poland. The SS provided the excuse. SS officers, disguised as Polish soldiers, took over a German radio station on the Polish border. They broadcast a message in Polish, attacking Hitler.

It was just a pantomime. The rest of the world was meant to think that war was justified. In fact, Hitler had signed the papers ordering an attack eight hours earlier. At dawn on 1 September 1939, German troops moved into Poland. Two days later, Britain and France declared war on Germany. The Second World War had begun.

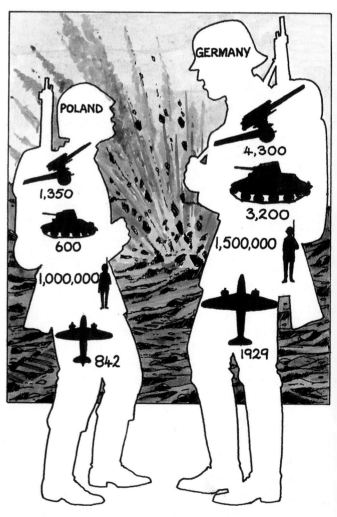

B How the German and Polish forces compared.

28

C War has begun and this young Polish girl finds the body of her elder sister, killed in a German air-raid.

D William Shirer described how ordinary Germans reacted to news of the war in his diary, published in 1941.

I was standing in the Wilhelmplatz about noon when the loud-speakers suddenly announced that England had declared herself at war with Germany. Some 250 people were standing there in the sun. They listened to the announcement. When it was finished, there was not a murmur. They just stood there as they were before. Stunned.

In 1914, I believe, the excitement in Berlin on the first day of the World War was tremendous. To-day, no excitement, no hurrahs, no cheering, no throwing of flowers, no war fever.

1 Look carefully at the following list.
  i) The Treaty of Versailles;
  ii) Hitler's desire for *lebensraum*;
  iii) the policy of appeasement;
  iv) the attack on Poland.
  a) Take each one in turn and explain whether it helped to cause the Second World War or not.
  b) Look back through this book. Write down any other causes that you can think of.
  c) Write down the short-term cause of the war. Explain how you chose it.
  d) Which do you think was the most important cause? Give reasons.

2 Please write a detailed answer. What caused the Second World War?

A WORD ABOUT PROPAGANDA

A. A wartime postcard.

Propaganda is an attempt to spread ideas and beliefs – and to get people to believe them. The aim is to control people's feelings and make them act in a certain way. Anything which does this is propaganda.

In the Great War, British propaganda had been very successful. One man studied carefully what the British had done. His name was Josef Goebbels. In 1933, he became the Nazi propaganda chief.

He had complete control over German radio, films and newspapers. Papers printed what he wanted them to print; cinemas screened the films he wanted Germans to see. Much of what they read or saw was propaganda.

After the war began, the British government set up the Ministry of Information. Its job was to produce propaganda for the British people. Another organisation produced propaganda aimed at the enemy.

So you need to study every wartime source with great care. Posters were always propaganda. Even photographs which showed real events could be used as propaganda. So were news bulletins. These pages contain just a few examples.

B. Truth and fiction. Above: British and German claims of planes shot down up to 31 October 1940. Below: the true figures.

C From *Mein Kampf* by Adolf Hitler (1924).
The understanding of the masses is very small and their intelligence is feeble. They quickly forget. All effective propaganda must be kept to a very few facts and must express these as far as possible in slogans. These slogans must be repeated constantly until the very last member of the public understands what you want him to understand by your slogan. Propaganda [must take a] one-sided attitude towards every question it deals with.

Don't forget that walls have ears!

CARELESS TALK COSTS LIVES

D One of the many British wartime posters which used this slogan.

A SQUADRON OF "COVENANTER" TANKS GOING INTO ACTION.

E A British wartime postcard. In fact, the Covenanter tank did not go into action. It was only used in Britain for training.

The lies you are being told!

« Those who do not know what they are fighting for ought to know at least what they are fighting **against** »

this is the main idea in allied propaganda. And this is why they are doing everything they can in order to make you, the soldiers, hate the Germans as much as possible. Creating hatred is the best way of inciting men to fight. thousands of you have already fallen victims to this artificially stirred hatred against the Germans.

In order to compel you to fight to the last even in the most hopeless situation your officers are telling you all sorts of tales of the terrible things which are awaiting you in case you are taken prisoners.

These are nothing but lies!

First lie: The Germans are treating the allied POW very badly and are not giving them anything to eat.

This lie hardly needs any refutation: Many of you have received letters from relatives or pals in German camps. You know the truth: Allied POW are being treated well and decently.

Second lie: The Germans are fanatics in matters of race, this is why they kill all their coloured or Indian prisoners.

What is true is that the Germans hate the Jews who have plotted this war for the sake of business. But even the Jewish POW (there are rare cases, though, because Jews are practically never fighting in the front lines) are being treated in accordance with the provisions of the Geneva Convention. Nobody in Germany feels any hatred against the coloured POW, and besides, Germany is on very friendly terms with the Indian people and its great leaders Gandhi, Jinnah and Subhas Chandra Bose.

Third lie: The Germans are forcing the allied POW into dangerous jobs at the front like clearing away mines, building fortifications etc.

A particularly silly lie, because if the POW would be used at the front every one of them would have to have an escort. Besides, such

F A German leaflet dropped on British troops during the war.

Each side used propaganda during the war. Although propaganda cannot be trusted, we can learn a great deal from it. For instance, propaganda can show us what governments wanted people to think.

1   a) Do you think the postcard in source A was made by the British or the Germans? Give reasons.
b) What are the aims of this postcard?

2   a) Look at source B. Why did each government not tell the truth?
b) If the radio figures were not true, how are the figures useful to a historian?
c) If the figures are not true, what does that tell you about source A?

3   a) Look at source D. What message is it giving?
b) Read source C. Do you think Hitler would have thought that source D was effective propaganda?
c) Why do you think the British government issued the photograph in source E?
d) Why did the Germans drop the leaflet in source F?

4   It is September 1939 and Poland has been invaded. Design a British propaganda poster which refers to this event.

THE SECOND WORLD WAR

| 1920 | 1930 | 1940 | 1950 | 1960 | 1970 |

Evacuation

Between 1 June and 3 September 1939, more than three and a half million Britons moved house. Many were newly-weds, moving into their first home. More people were getting married than at any other time in history.

But many of those moving were children. In the three days before war started, one and a half million children left London and other major cities to live somewhere safer. It was called *evacuation*. These children were accompanied by their teachers. Mothers were only allowed to go too if their children were under five.

The rest were not even allowed onto station platforms to say good-bye. They did not know where their children were going – or whether they would ever see them again.

All these evacuees had to live somewhere. Anyone with space to spare had to house at least one child. You could not argue about it. In return, the government paid you 52½p a week.

On arrival, local people chose their evacuees. These new 'foster parents' were often fairly well-off middle-class people. Few had ever seen such poor, dirty children before. Many of them came from the poorest parts of big cities.

B The government said that the children should take these possessions with them.

In Stepney, London, only 10 per cent of homes had a proper bath; in Glasgow, there was a bath in only half the homes. Many children were filthy; about half had lice or fleas. Some of them brought just one set of clothes – for daytime *and* night-time.

Their new 'parents' soon found that the children's behaviour was not what they expected, either. About one in ten evacuees had not been toilet-trained. Some were used to urinating on the floor. One girl even fried her host's tropical fish to eat; they were worth £25.

Many children came from large families living in small houses. At home, they had had to share a bed. Given a bed of their own, some chose to sleep underneath it. One was found fast asleep, standing up in a corner of the room. He did not know what the bed was for.

But evacuation had important consequences. For the first time, the well-off knew how the poor lived. The experience left them shocked and saddened. Many people felt guilty that British children should live in such poverty. Before the war was over, the government was planning a better future for them.

A This boy was from the first school to start evacuation at 5.30 am on 1 September 1939.

C Bernard Kops was sent to Buckinghamshire with his sister (1963).

Everything was so clean in the room. We were even given flannels and toothbrushes. We'd never cleaned our teeth up till then. And hot water came from the tap. And there was a lavatory upstairs. And carpets. And something called an eiderdown. And clean sheets. This was all very odd. And rather scaring.

D One evacuee wrote home to his mother.

They call this 'spring', mum, and they have one down here every year.

OLD MAID: "IF THERE'S A WAR I'M GOING TO HAVE SIX CHILDREN!"

BILLETING OF CHILDREN

A "BAMFORTH" COMIC

G Postcards were making fun of evacuation even before war broke out (1938).

H In 1985, an Essex evacuee recalled her experience. (The 'witch' is the old lady she stayed with.)

About once a month my parents sent me a large food parcel, in answer to a frantic cry for food. The first time, I was allowed to keep the contents. But the 'witch' had seen the goodies I'd received. No sooner was the next one delivered than on went a sticky label, addressed to her daughter in Birmingham.

On another occasion, I received a scooter from my father. One or two scoots up and down the garden path were all I managed to get before that, too, was rewrapped and shipped off to her daughter's children.

Our interpretation of the past is based on sources. However, two sources can often give quite different ideas of what happened. So the sources which a historian uses will affect the interpretation he or she gives of the past.

E The *Daily Mirror* of 4 September 1939 gave this picture the caption, 'Aren't they happy?'

F In 1990, Dorothy Harmsworth recalled her experience as an evacuee.

This old lady and gentleman got me. They were extremely strict. If you dropped a crumb on the tablecloth, you didn't have any more tea – that was it, and we went to bed. I was put in this great big bedroom. On the top [of the wardrobe] was a statue of Jesus with his arms held out. The reflection of this used to shine up and it frightened me to death.

And, of course, I used to wet myself. I was frightened – and the next day my pyjama trousers used to be hung around my neck. That was their way. I used to go across the road to my brother – they were living like pigs and enjoying every moment of it. The people they were with didn't care what they did.

1 a) Why were children evacuated?
   b) Look at what the boy is carrying in the cartoon on page 32. Why did he need each of these things?
   c) Do you think all children took these things? Explain your answer.

2 a) Study sources C, D and E. Write down what idea of evacuation they give.
   b) Study sources A, F and H. Write down what idea of evacuation they give.
   c) Explain why you have such different answers.
   d) Why might source E be unreliable?

3 a) Pick any one of the children in the sources. Describe what you think they felt and thought about being evacuated.
   b) Do you think all children felt like this? Please give detailed reasons for your answer.

THE HOME FRONT

A Cinemas shut when war broke out but they soon opened again. *Gone With the Wind* was one of the most popular wartime films.

Most British people feared air raids more than anything else. It wasn't only children who were evacuated at the start of the war. So were some animals from London Zoo. Others were less lucky: over 200 snakes were killed on 31 August.

People were afraid of gas attacks, too. Pillar box tops were given a fresh coat of paint which was sensitive to gas. Everybody was told to carry a gas mask at all times; at first, they did. But a check in November showed that a third of gas mask boxes only contained sandwiches.

There were other changes at the start of the war. On 1 September, the television service closed down and the blackout began the same evening. Street and shop lights were turned off. Anyone with a light shining in their house could be taken to court. Shops in Glasgow sold 8 miles (13 km) of blackout material in a single day.

On 3 September, all men aged 18 to 41 were called up to fight. Anyone whose job was vital in the war was not included, and conscientious objectors were not forced to join up.

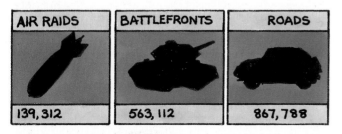

AIR RAIDS	BATTLEFRONTS	ROADS
139,312	563,112	867,788

B Casualty figures, September 1939 to September 1944.

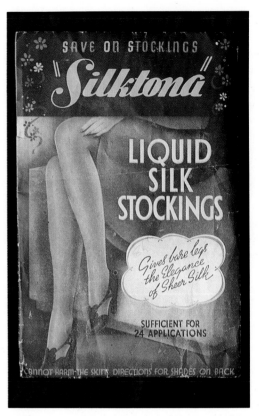

C Silk stockings became rare. Manufacturers persuaded women to paint their legs instead. Gravy browning was a cheaper substitute.

One thing did not change in September 1939. You could still buy as much food as you could afford. But Britain imported over half her food and some foreign foods were soon hard to find. Lemons became so rare that they were auctioned!

It was January 1940 before the government introduced rationing . Each person had a ration book and used it to buy a limited amount of bacon, sugar and butter. Meat and tea were rationed later in 1940; jam was added in 1941 and sweets were rationed in 1942.

Restaurants were not affected at the start. So the rich could still each much as they wished. It was 1942 before the government rationed restaurants. They were only allowed to serve one main course – and the meal could not cost more than 25p.

Everyone was afraid of air raids but, at first, the bombers did not come. So the government relaxed some of its new rules. On the streets, the blackout was made less strict although street lights were still dim. Pedestrians were allowed to use torches at night, as long as they were covered with tissue paper.

When the bombs did not fall, many mothers wanted their children back from the countryside. By 1940, nearly half of the evacuees were home again. As someone said, they'd rather have bombs falling on them than apples.

D The *Daily Mirror* printed this advice from the government on 4 September 1939.

Keep off the streets as much as possible.

Carry your gas mask with you always.

Make sure every member of your household have on them their names and addresses clearly written.

Sew a label on children's clothing so that they cannot pull it off.

Churches and other places of public worship will not be closed.

All day schools in evacuation areas in England, Wales and Scotland are to be closed for lessons for at least a week from yesterday.

In the reception areas schools will be opened as soon as evacuation is complete.

E The same newspaper reported that:

A pleasant surprise awaited more than 1,000 short-term prisoners in three London gaols during the weekend. They were released. [They] were given travelling vouchers to return to their homes.

At Wandsworth Prison, 400 prisoners were told they had been pardoned. They were released in batches of twenty and were given [25p] each. Men with longer sentences were transferred to another prison.

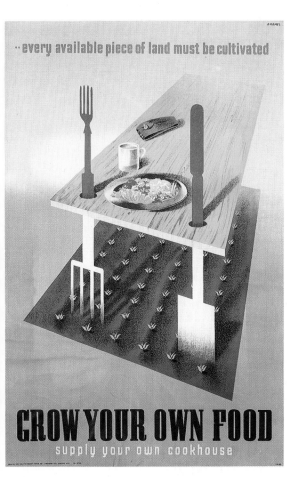

F Government posters encouraged people to grow food to make up for shortages . . .

Home Grown

G . . . and picture postcards made jokes about it.

Some changes are sudden; some take longer to happen. Britain was at war from 3 September 1939 but life in Britain did not completely change overnight.

1 Read sources D and E.
   a) Which changes did the newspaper report?
   b) Which things stayed the same?
2 Read page 34.
   a) Which changes happened rapidly?
   b) Which changes came more slowly?
3 'Food was rationed in January 1940.' Is this statement true or not? Please give a detailed answer.

CHURCHILL TAKES OVER

A Horse transport was no match for air attack. Scenes like this were common in 1939-40.

The new world war was very different from the last one. This time, the Germans used the tactic of blitzkrieg which means *lightning war*. This involved sudden and massive use of tanks and planes.

Britain and France had promised to stand by Poland but there was nothing they could do. German troops took control of western Poland and Russian troops invaded in the east. By the end of September 1939, Poland no longer existed.

Back home, the British and French waited for the bombs to fall. But there were no bombs and very little fighting in the winter of 1939-40. People called it a 'Phoney War'. In April 1940, Chamberlain even told the British people that 'Hitler had missed the bus'.

He was wrong. Within days, Germany invaded Denmark and Norway. On 10 May, Chamberlain was forced to resign and Winston Churchill became the new British Prime Minister. That same day, German tanks rolled into Holland and Belgium. Days later, Churchill was telling MPs, 'I have nothing to offer but blood, toil, tears and sweat.'

By the end of May, Holland, Belgium and Luxembourg had surrendered. Meanwhile, the Germans were attacking France. A British Expeditionary Force had been sent to France but the German advance continued. So the British troops retreated to the Channel coast.

At Dunkirk, French and British forces were surrounded. Over 300,000 of them were rescued by sea and the newspapers called it 'a miracle'. But Britain had been forced to withdraw.

On 14 June, German troops marched into Paris. By then, Italy, too, had declared war, although its troops were using rifles designed in 1891. On 22 June, France surrendered to Germany. The agreement was signed in the same railway carriage in which the Germans themselves had agreed to end the Great War.

Britain alone now faced Germany. Her European allies were defeated; the United States stayed neutral. Hitler hoped that Britain, too, would surrender. But Churchill vowed to fight on. It meant that Hitler's next step would be to attack Britain. The British did not have to wait long.

HOLDING THE LINE!

B Churchill had not supported appeasement. This 1942 American poster shows him as a British bulldog. The cigar became Churchill's trademark. However, one colleague said that 'his use of matches outstripped his consumption of cigars'.

What happened at Dunkirk?

C After the retreat: British equipment abandoned on the Dunkirk beach.

D L E Snellgrove: *The Modern World since 1870* (a textbook, 1968).
An armada of pleasure boats, yachts and dinghies set out from the south coast to rescue [the troops].

E *The World To-day*, another textbook (1958).
The sea was calm. Some of the men on the sand-dunes played cricket as the German bombers flew overhead and the shells from the German army fell among them. In all 337,130 British and French soldiers were taken to safety. Mr Churchill rightly said this great defeat was really a great victory because it [allowed] Britain to continue the great fight.

F Nicholas Harman: *The Necessary Myth* (1990).
[People believe] that an armada of civilian 'little ships' played [an important] part in the rescue of the army. This was false. The little ships operated only on the last two days of the British evacuation. Civilian volunteers could not have come forward earlier, since the whole [event] was kept secret from the public until three-quarters of the army was home.

G Clive Ponting: *1940: Myth and Reality* (1990).
Over the last four days, the small boats helped lift 26,000 troops from the beaches, about eight per cent of the total evacuated.

H The *Daily Express* printed this on 31 May 1940.
The B.E.F. carry out the greatest rear-guard action ever fought in history. Brave men face a mass of metal and machinery. Yet such is their [bravery] that Hitler has to throw a million troops against them.
When our last soldiers reach these shores, they must be treated as a victorious army. The glory won by our Army is shared by the Navy and the Royal Air Force.

I Clive Ponting: *1940: Myth and Reality* (1990).
General Alexander was shocked by the behaviour of the soldiers. During a secret session of the House of Commons, several MPs told how a large number of officers had run away and deserted their troops so as to get on to the earliest boat. In private, Churchill told ministers that Dunkirk was 'the greatest British military defeat for many centuries.'

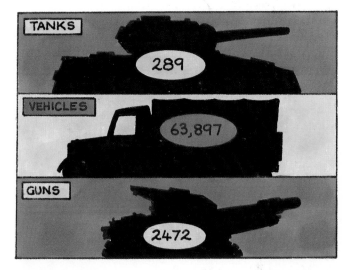

TANKS 289
VEHICLES 63,897
GUNS 2472

J Equipment left behind at Dunkirk.

1 a) What was blitzkrieg?
b) Which country was defeated in 1939?
c) Which countries were defeated in 1940?

2 a) Read the sources on this page. According to Churchill, was Dunkirk a victory or a defeat? Explain your answer.
b) Was he stating a fact or giving his point of view? Explain how you decided.
c) Suggest reasons why sources H and I disagree.
d) How does source H give a false picture of what happened?

3 a) The sources give two different versions of what happened at Dunkirk. Write a brief summary of each version in your own words. In each case, say which sources you used.
b) Which version do you think is more accurate? Explain in detail how you decided.
c) How did the circumstances of the time affect what was written in source H?

THE BLITZ

Before German troops could cross the Channel, Hitler had to destroy the RAF. In August, the Battle of Britain began when the Luftwaffe attacked airfields in south-east England. Goering boasted that he would have control of the air within four days.

The raids *did* damage the RAF. At one point, pilots were being killed faster than new ones were being trained. But the RAF had an advantage over the Germans: it had radar. This meant the RAF could spot invading aircraft up to 17 miles (27km) away. The Germans had to fly unguided.

Later in August, the RAF bombed Berlin and Goering changed his tactics. He decided to bomb cities instead. In September, London became the main target.

The bombers came, night after night, for 76 nights in all. There was just one night off when bad weather stopped the flights. Londoners called it 'the blitz', short for *blitzkrieg*.

George helps out. London Zoo's camel was used to help clear rubble during the Blitz.

At first, the RAF was too short of planes to offer much defence. But, soon, the British were building more planes than the Germans were destroying. In the air, British Spitfires and Hurricanes fought dog-fights with German bombers. German losses mounted.

The Luftwaffe was trying to bomb London into giving up. But Londoners grew used to spending their nights in shelters or underground. Queues formed at dawn outside the tube stations for a place the next night.

A Furniture and other belongings saved from blitz-damaged homes in London.

In September, Hitler gave up all plans to invade Britain. But the Blitz went on. From November onwards, other cities were bombed. That month, the centre of Coventry was destroyed.

During the winter of 1940-41, Hitler and Mussolini launched attacks elsewhere. Italian troops had little success. In September 1940, they attacked Egypt but the British forced them to retreat. An attack on Greece in October was no more successful.

By May 1941, British and Empire forces had taken over Mussolini's first conquest, Abyssinia. By then, the German army was having to help the Italians. In April, Germany bombed Greece; it surrendered within a month.

Meanwhile, the blitz of Britain went on. 'Business as usual,' was a favourite phrase. But civilian casualties mounted and, at times, the people's spirits sank. Civilian casualties outnumbered military ones until September 1942.

On 10 May 1941, 1436 people died in London alone. It was the city's worst night. It was also the last. During the summer, raids grew fewer. In June, Germany had a new enemy: the Soviet Union.

Could London hold out?

B Ed Murrow was an American journalist working in London. This is from a broadcast of September 1940.

How long the people of this city can stand this sort of thing, I don't know. I know only that they are not near their limit. Most of them expect the worst to come.

C Quentin Reynolds was another American journalist in London during the Blitz. This is what he told Americans in a film commentary.

I am a neutral reporter. I can assure you – there is no panic, no fear, no despair in London Town. There is nothing but determination, confidence and courage among the people of Churchill's island.

It is true that the Nazis will be over again tomorrow night, and the night after that, and every night. They will drop thousands of bombs. But a bomb has its limitations. It can only destroy buildings and kill people. It cannot kill the unconquerable spirit and courage of the people of London.

D Joseph Kennedy was US Ambassador to Britain. On 27 September 1940, he wrote:

My feeling is that [the British] are in a bad way. I [have no] confidence in the conduct of this war. I was delighted to see that the president said he was not going to enter the war.

F Pilot Roy Marchand was killed in September 1940. But his photograph went on being used in this famous poster.

G Churchill praised the RAF in a speech to Parliament:

Never in the field of human conflict was so much owed by so many to so few.

When dealing with wartime sources, we must constantly watch out for propaganda. A poster is clearly propaganda but other ways of influencing people are not so obvious.

E Children sheltering from bombs during the Battle of Britain. A copy was hung in the British Embassy in the United States.

1 a) What was the Luftwaffe?
 b) Why did it bomb (i) southern airfields and (ii) London?

2 a) Read sources B, C and D. How do they differ?
 b) Mr Reynolds said he was a 'neutral' reporter. Was this true? Give reasons.
 c) How reliable do you think source C is? Give reasons.
 d) Why were the views of Mr Kennedy (source D) important?
 e) What were Americans supposed to think when they saw source E?

4 a) Think carefully. Which of these sources are propaganda? Explain how you decided.
 b) Look at source A. Write a caption for this photograph to appear in a British newspaper.
 c) Write a caption to appear in a German newspaper.

HITLER ATTACKS THE USSR

A The German attack on the USSR. It was codenamed Barbarossa, meaning *red beard*.

The Russian dictator Joseph Stalin had a policy of getting rid of anyone he thought was a threat. Between 1938 and 1941, about one-third of all army officers were killed. Yet Stalin was worried. Germany needed food and oil – and the USSR had plenty. It could be Hitler's next target.

In the spring of 1941, Churchill actually warned Stalin that an attack was coming. Nevertheless, Stalin set off on his summer holidays in June. Days later, on 22 June, the attack came. Three million German troops moved into the Soviet Union. It was the biggest invasion in history.

War had come to the USSR: Stalin called it the Great Patriotic War. But some Russians did not feel patriotic about it. Many were delighted to welcome German soldiers: they hoped that Hitler would get rid of Stalin. Thousands of troops did not even bother to fight.

But Churchill supported Stalin. In July, Britain and the USSR signed an agreement; they promised to fight together until the Germans were beaten.

But Stalin was desperate. In October, he offered to give Hitler huge areas of land in return for peace. Hitler refused: he was convinced the Germans would win.

By Christmas 1941, it looked as though they might: half of the Russian coal and wheat production was under German control. Leningrad was surrounded; German soldiers were fighting in the suburbs of Moscow.

However, two factors worked against the Germans. First, Stalin used a 'scorched earth' policy: this meant that retreating Soviet troops destroyed anything which might help the Germans.

Second, the Germans were not ready for the Russian winter. The temperature around Leningrad sank to −38°C. Inside the city, people ate rats and dogs. Outside, German tanks broke down and soldiers shivered in their summer clothing; more died from cold than from bullets.

Despite the danger, Stalin went on getting rid of people he thought were against him. Many were sent to labour camps. In 1942, there were actually as many prisoners in labour camps as there were soldiers fighting the Germans. And their death rate was about the same.

B This German tank crew had to thaw the mud around the tank before they could use it.

The siege of Leningrad

F Calories per person per day in Leningrad. Nearly 4000 people starved to death on Christmas Day 1941.

C Death from cold and hunger became a common sight in the streets of Leningrad. Pieces of unburied bodies sometimes went missing; so did small children.

D This is from the diary of Mikhail Tikhomirov, a teenager living in Leningrad. In 1941, the Germans began a siege of the town which lasted until 1944. Mikhail himself was killed by a shell in 1942.

8 December 1941. School has no coal for heating. We have our lessons in the air raid shelter, because the classrooms are desperately cold, with their windows blown out by shells. At home, we live in one room to save heat.

We eat twice a day – morning and evening. Always soup and rather thin. Cocoa in the morning, coffee in the evening. We've bought 5kg of carpenter's glue and make jellies from it, and we eat them with mustard.

21 December. My birthday went well. We [had] our birthday meal – two dishes of thick cabbage soup, then a [soup] of peas, soya and noodles. I don't think I've ever eaten anything so tasty. With the coffee there was a slice of boiled kidney, a slice of tinned cod, bread and honey.

25 December. Today my sister didn't go to school because she had a cough, but mainly to save her strength.

E Olga Rybakov described December 1942, when temperatures were −40°C (1991).

People began to starve and die from cold. Always when I went to find food, I had to pass dead bodies – then, on my way back, some more.

G Stalin's scorched earth policy: these peasants save their grain as their village burns.

1 a) Copy the map on page 40.
b) How far did the Germans have to travel to get to Moscow?
c) Why would this cause them problems?

2 Study the sources on Leningrad.
a) How can you tell from source D that the city is under siege?
b) What picture of life in Leningrad do you get from the sources?
c) Which one do you think best shows the suffering of the people? Give reasons for your choice.
d) You are a German soldier in the USSR. Write a postcard home to your parents. Remember that your mail may be censored.

PEARL HARBOR

A American ships under attack at Pearl Harbor, 7 December 1941.

When war began, the United States did not join in. But the American President, Franklin Roosevelt, did help the British. In March 1941, the USA introduced the 'Lend-Lease' scheme; materials would be lent to Britain, as long as Britain paid for them later.

In August 1941, Roosevelt and Churchill met secretly at sea and drew up the Atlantic Charter. It stated what they would do when Germany was beaten.

Meanwhile, in the east, Japan had been expanding. When war began, they saw their chance to attack British and other colonies in the Pacific. They claimed they were freeing them. In fact, they were after raw materials – oil, tin, rice and rubber. Only one country could stop them capturing these areas: the United States.

So the Japanese planned an attack on the American naval base on Hawaii. It was called Pearl Harbor. The aim was to destroy the US Pacific Fleet. The Japanese did not declare war on the USA: they wanted to surprise the Americans.

The attack was planned for 7 December 1941. With their radios off, the Japanese fleet steamed across the Pacific Ocean. For the Americans, it was the early hours of a normal Sunday morning. At 6.40am a submarine was spotted outside Pearl Harbor and the Americans fired at it. Yet the US commander did not call a general alert.

At 8.00am, the main wave of Japanese aeroplanes swooped on the base. Nearly 200 American planes were destroyed; another 159 were damaged. Five battleships were sunk or damaged; over 2400 people died.

Americans were shocked. It seemed to be a stunning success for the Japanese. But the Japanese had missed the American aircraft carriers, which were at sea at the time. They had also failed to destroy stocks of oil.

However, the attack brought the USA into the war. On 8 December, the USA declared war on Japan – and Hitler declared war on the USA. It was now truly a world war.

> How much of a surprise was the attack on Pearl Harbor? Did Churchill or Roosevelt know an attack was coming? Did any Americans know that Pearl Harbor was the target?

B Map showing Japanese conquests in 1941-42.

Japanese May Strike Over Weekend!

The Honolulu Sunday Advertiser
Hawaii's Territorial Newspaper

FINAL EDITION

CLIPPER MAIL SCHEDULE
From Coast—Phil. Clip., Mon., 7 a.m.
To Coast—Calif. Clip., Sun., 11 a.m.
From Orient—Ch. Clip., Thurs., 4 p.m.
To Orient—Phil. Clip., Mon., 9 p.m.
From N. Z.—Pac. Clip., Dec. 10, 4 p.m.
To N. Z.—Pac. Clip., Tues., 9 p.m.

86TH. YEAR, NO. 19,759.— 62 PAGES — To Reach All Departments TELEPHONE 2311 — HONOLULU, HAWAII, U. S. A. SUNDAY MORNING, NOVEMBER 30, 1941. Weather: New York, 40; Chicago, 44; Honolulu, 65; San Francisco, 54. PRICE TEN CENTS

KURUSU BLUNTLY WARNED NATION READY FOR BATTLE

C Headline from the *Honolulu Advertiser before* the attack. The report was by the journalist quoted in source F.

D Long afterwards, American posters reminded people of Pearl Harbor (1944).

Did America Know?

E This is from *The Second World War*, a school textbook (1976).
On December 7th 1941, the Japanese made a surprise attack on Pearl Harbor.

F An American journalist met Cornell Hull (US Secretary of State) on 29 November 1941. He later recalled:
He [told me] that Pearl Harbor would be attacked on December 7th. He emphasised December 7th. He pulled out of his pocket the [paper] which stated that Pearl Harbor would be attacked on December 7th.

G The President's wife, Eleanor Roosevelt, wrote about 7 December in her autobiography (1950).
Franklin sent word a short time before lunch that he could not possibly join us. He had been increasingly worried for some time. By the time lunch was over the news had come of the attack on Pearl Harbor. Later, [we] had a chance to talk. I thought that Franklin was more [calm] than he had appeared in a long time.

H In 1980, another American recalled a meeting with J Edgar Hoover (Head of the FBI) in early 1942.
[He] said that from early   fall   1941 they had had warnings that [an attack] was coming. President Roosevelt had had warnings from a number of sources but he was sure they were not passed on to the commanders in the Pacific. Hoover said the President told him not to mention to anyone any of this information.

I James Rusbridger investigated the event in *Betrayal at Pearl Harbor* (1991).
On the evidence in [this] book, we show that Churchill was aware that a task force had sailed from Japan in late November 1941, and that one of its likely targets was Pearl Harbor. Churchill deliberately kept this vital information from Roosevelt, because he realized an attack of this nature was a means of [getting] America into the war.

1 Put these events in the order in which they happened: (a) the Atlantic Charter; (b) the USA declared war on Japan; (c) the Lend-Lease scheme; (d) the attack on Pearl Harbor.

2 Read the sources on this page.
a) Write down any one opinion from these sources. Give a reason for your choice.
b) What evidence is there that Roosevelt did or didn't know an attack was coming?
c) How do sources E and F disagree?
d) Can you prove that either Churchill or Roosevelt knew that Pearl Harbor would be attacked? Explain your answer.

3 a) What two versions of the event can you get from these sources? Explain which sources support which version.
b) Which version do you think is more likely to be right? Please answer in detail.
c) Look at source D. Why was it important that the American public thought the attack was a surprise?

1942: THE WAR'S TURNING-POINTS

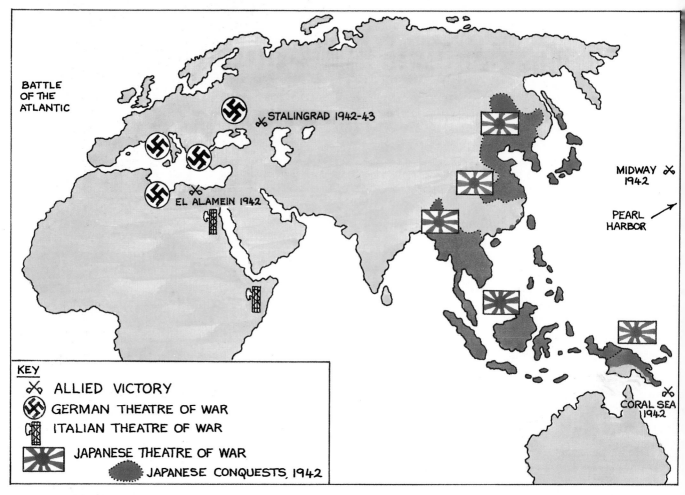

A The Second World War; where the fighting went on.

Right from the start, this had been more than just a European war. On the very first day of the war, a British liner was sunk. The Atlantic Ocean was a battleground from 1939 to 1945.

The Germans wanted to control the ocean to stop supplies getting into Britain. The aim was to starve Britain into giving up. The British government replied by using a convoy system.

Even so, the merchant ships took a battering from U-boats in 1941. They were being sunk faster than they could be built. The next year was also bad. But things improved in 1943. Naval ships were better equipped to hunt down the U-boats. At the same time, RAF long-range bombers kept watch over the merchant ships.

After Pearl Harbor, the Japanese continued their conquests in the Pacific. But the year 1942 proved a turning-point. In May, the Japanese had their first setback when the US fleet defeated them at the battle of the Coral Sea. The USA won an even more decisive victory in June at the battle of Midway.

The German advance into Russia also slowed down in 1942. Hitler changed his plan and German armies marched south towards the city of Stalingrad. They were heading for the Soviet oil fields. In September, German troops were actually fighting in Stalingrad itself.

But Stalin was determined to save the city which was named after him. Soviet troops defended the city, street by street. In November, the Russians counter-attacked; they cut the Germans off from their supply lines and surrounded them.

About 285,000 Germans were trapped. Hitler refused to let them surrender. So they fought on through a bitterly cold winter. By Christmas, they were cooking their horses for food. In February 1943, the German commander disobeyed Hitler and surrendered. Only 91,000 men had survived.

Meanwhile, the British had scored a success in North Africa. In October 1942, General Montgomery's 8th Army had attacked the German Afrika Korps at El Alamein.

The Germans were defeated and the British pushed them back westwards. When American troops landed in Algeria, the Germans were trapped. In May 1943, they, too, surrendered.

Stalingrad: Why did the Germans lose?

B John Martell: *The Twentieth Century World* (1969).

As winter advanced, the advantages came to be more on the Russian side: the German supply lines were stretched, and German losses were mounting. The Russians were able to receive supplies from the British, and from their own factories in the Urals.

C A message from the German army commander to Hitler (23 November 1942).

Our ammunition and petrol supplies are running out. Several anti-tank units have none left. Supplies not expected to reach them in time. Army heading for disaster if it does not succeed in pulling together all its strength to deal knockout blow against enemy. It is essential to withdraw from Stalingrad.

D Franz Halder, a German general, recalled:

A statement was read to [Hitler] which showed that Stalin would still be able to muster 1.25 million men in the region of Stalingrad. [It also] proved that the Russian output of tanks amounted to 1200 a month. Hitler flew at the man who was reading, with clenched fists and foam at the corners of his mouth. [He] forbade him to read such idiotic twaddle.

ПРЕВРАЩЕНИЕ „ФРИЦЕВ"

ТО НЕ ЗВЕРИ С ДИКИМ БОЕМ
В БУРНЫЙ РИНУЛИСЬ ПОТОК,
ЭТО ГИТЛЕР СТРОЙ ЗА СТРОЕМ
ГОНИТ „ФРИЦЕВ" НА ВОСТОК.

ЗДЕСЬ, ГДЕ ОКНА ВСЕ — БОЙНИЦЫ,
ЗДЕСЬ, ГДЕ СМЕРТЬ ТАЯТ КУСТЫ,
ЗДЕСЬ, ГЛОТНУВ ЧУЖОЙ ЗЕМЛИЦЫ,
ОДУРАЧЕННЫЕ „ФРИЦЫ"
ПРЕВРАЩАЮТСЯ В КРЕСТЫ.

ГИБЕЛЬ СВОЛОЧИ НЕМЕЦКОЙ
НЕ ЧЬЕ — ЛИБО КОЛДОВСТВО,
ЭТО — АРМИИ СОВЕТСКОЙ
БОЕВОЕ ТОРЖЕСТВО!

E This 1942 Soviet cartoon showed Hitler leading his men towards the Russian winter.

F Felt boots were issued to German sentries. These Russian soldiers are joking about them.

G The Russian commander, General Zhukov, later wrote:

The Germans could not stand close fighting; they [used] their automatic weapons from well over half a mile away, when their bullets could not cover half the distance. They fired simply to keep up their morale.

Historians ask: 'Why were the Germans defeated at Stalingrad? What caused it?' Of course, there was a number of causes. So historians try to discover the most important causes. They also try to work out how the causes are connected.

1. a) Which victories did the Allies win in 1942?
   b) Why did the Germans attack British ships in the Atlantic?
   c) Why were German submarines less successful after 1943?

2. Study the sources on this page. Please write your answers in complete sentences.
   a) List all the reasons why the German army was defeated at Stalingrad.
   b) Which do you think was the main cause or causes? Explain how you decided.
   c) Is there anything you think these sources do not explain?
   d) Write an essay, explaining why the German army was beaten. Take care to explain how the different causes were connected to each other.

BRITISH WOMEN AT WAR

OGDEN'S CIGARETTES

REMOVAL OF INCENDIARY BOMB WITH SCOOP AND HOE

OGDEN'S CIGARETTES

TWO-MEN PORTABLE MANUAL FIRE-PUMP IN ACTION

OGDEN'S CIGARETTES

A CHAIN OF BUCKETS

A Cigarette cards showed that women were expected to do new household chores.

In 1941, the government decided to call up unmarried women, aged 20-30. Britain was the first nation in modern history to do this. Women soon showed they could do any job which a man could do. Some joined one of the services, such as the WAAF . The rest went into the Land Army or industry.

This offered women new opportunities. Before the war, many women had been household servants. They met few people; their hours were long and the pay was poor.

Factories offered better pay for shorter hours. But few pre-war factories had employed women on the shop floor. It was a while before the men got used to it. At first, many were quick to take the mickey.

The bosses, too, had to adapt. The men had accepted dirty toilets and no rest rooms. Women wanted something better. As a result of their campaigns, everybody benefited.

One thing did not change. Men still earned more than women doing the same job. In 1939, an injured female defence worker got less compensation than a male: she was valued at just two-thirds of a man.

The war brought women other freedoms, too. Some don't seem very important now. For instance, clothes were soon in short supply. So, in 1942, women were allowed to go to church services without wearing hats or stockings. Older people were quite shocked.

Relationships with men were more relaxed during the war and more unmarried women had sexual relationships. As one woman said, 'We all thought we hadn't much longer to live, so why not get what we could out of life?'

Despite the changes, many people still held traditional views of men and women. In 1944, the BBC banned a song called, 'I heard you cried last night'. The BBC thought the idea of a man crying was bad for morale.

Some men resented women's new freedoms. Plenty of men still thought that a woman's real place was in the home. When war ended, many women found that it was. The men returned from the war and were given their old jobs back. But this did not last. Many women had grown used to having their own career – and the new freedoms.

INSIDE INFORMATION

B Picture postcards showed women (and girls) still doing traditional women's jobs.

G This letter was written to *Woman's Own* in 1941.

My husband has just been on leave; for 5 months I have had baby tying me hand and foot. Now my husband has gone back [cross] because I told him he ought to get up and light the fire; he even asked me to clean his army boots for him, which is a job no woman should be asked to do. He will be home again in 3 months; how can I make him see his duty?

H And this was the answer she got from the Agony Aunt (1941).

You [are] wanting him to wait on you hand and foot when he gets a much needed rest. You ought to be ashamed of yourself, my dear. Next leave, show how pleased you are to have him home again. It would be nice if you gave him his breakfast in bed. Make every moment one he can look back on happily for months to come.

I Women of the ATS on an anti-aircraft gun site.

C A woman working on an under-carriage.

Sources D-F come from *A People's War*, 1986.

D Ellen McCulloch was a union official.

Even in 1942 you'd ask a girl did she like the job and she'd say, 'Oh yes, I never thought I'd be able to do it. After all, it's not women's work, is it?' They had [the idea] that women's work was done by inferior people. But they began to realise that they weren't second-class citizens.

E Joan Hughes delivered brand new planes to the RAF. She recalled:

There were masses of letters from women saying how dare we fly? We should be at home cooking our husband's dinner.

F Mona Marshall had been a nursemaid. In the war, she worked in a steelworks.

The war was the best thing that ever happened to us. My generation had been taught to do as we were told. At work you did exactly as your boss told you; then you went home to do exactly what your husband told you. The war changed all that. The war made me stand on my own two feet.

---

1 a) List all the changes in women's lives which happened during the war.
   b) What evidence is there that some people's attitudes did not change? Give examples.
   c) Which of the changes was economic?
   d) Did everyone think that the changes brought progress? Explain your answer.

2 a) How useful are the pictures for understanding women's lives in the war?
   b) Which one is most useful for understanding how home life changed? Give careful reasons.

3 a) What ideas and attitudes are shown by (i) the women and (ii) the men in the sources? Please write a detailed answer.
   b) Why do you think they had these attitudes?

LIFE IN HITLER'S EUROPE

A This German postcard joked about rations. The menu includes 'foot rags with fleas' and sparrows.

While the British coped with ration books, so did the Germans. By 1941, the basic German diet was bread, potatoes and cabbage. Milk was for children only. Butter was scarce so most people ate margarine: they called it 'Hitler's butter'.

Food was scarce in all countries conquered by Germany. Even in Paris, well-dressed people could be seen scavenging in dustbins by the middle of the war. In Poland and the Soviet Union, it was even worse.

Hitler did not look upon Poles and Russians as human beings. Living standards in Poland were kept as low as possible. In 1943, the Germans confiscated the Soviet harvest: Russians were sub-human so they didn't need food.

In each occupied country, Nazi officials controlled every aspect of local life. The most feared Nazis of all were the SS and the Gestapo (the secret police). They treated all foreigners with great cruelty. Once again, the Poles and Russians suffered the most.

Hitler had ordered that German soldiers could not be put on trial for anything done to Russians. So, whole families were arrested and shot. Their homes and possessions were burned. Every time a German soldier died in the Soviet Union, up to 100 Communists were shot in revenge.

Near Smolensk, the Germans shot about 200 schoolchildren, after raping some of the girls. In Lvov, members of the Hitler Youth movement used local children for target practice. One teenager was shot just for singing an anti-German song.

Russian prisoners-of-war were treated no better. Nearly 6 million of them were captured – but only about 2 million survived. Torture was common: they had eyes and finger-nails torn out; arms and legs were hacked off. In winter, prisoners' clothing was taken away so they would die of cold. Others simply starved to death.

Throughout Europe, 5 million people were rounded up and taken to Germany in cattle trucks. They worked in factories or in slave labour camps. These camps were filthy; badly-fed workers worked long hours. Many never returned home.

The same was true of some children. The German ideal was to have blonde hair and blue eyes. So some fair-haired children were taken back to Germany and brought up as Germans. Ones with dark hair ended up in labour camps.

B The Nazis' ideal girl is shown in this pre-war German poster.

C This German woman seems delighted with her new ration book.

D Anyone listening to BBC radio could be put to death. A German teenager, Ilse Koehn, listened secretly with a friend in 1944. (From *Mischling, Second Degree*, 1978).

'My father and I put this radio together,' he says proudly. 'You'll have to promise not to tell anyone, not *anyone*, about what you're going to hear. If my watch is right, we should catch it. Here it is! Listen!'

'Boom-boom-boomboom. London calling. London calling.'

We have to listen very hard to catch any words over the other noises. Eberhard circles areas on the map. It is already full of marks. When the broadcast is over, he says, 'As usual, our newscasts are way off. See here! Strasbourg fell on November 23, Saarlautern on December 3. Yet this very morning Goebbels said that we are still holding out heroically.'

In 1940, Germans were told they could only take baths on Saturdays and Sundays.

E This Russian medical orderly remembered a German air attack in the winter of 1942-43 (1991).

I knew how cruelly the Germans treated our people. I experienced it myself. A driver and I were in charge of an ambulance filled with wounded. The road was bombed and the aircraft began to circle and rake us with fire. There was a ploughed field with a heap of stones in one corner. I dashed away from the road and lay down by the stones.

It seemed to me that he flew so low I thought he was bound to crash. He could see that it was a girl lying there, too. I had long blonde hair. Well, why did he do that? Or take another example – once they set up a row of boots in front of our trenches. [These] boots belonged to our soldiers, with their cut-off legs still in them.

F Many civilians who worked against the Germans were publicly hanged (1942).

1 Please answer in complete sentences.
 a) Why did Germans treat Russians and Poles so badly?
 b) Why do you think Communists were shot if a German soldier died?
 c) Why were fair-haired children sometimes taken back to Germany?

2 a) Look at sources A and C. Which one do you think is more useful for understanding German feelings about rationing? Give reasons for your choice.
 b) Do you think source C is reliable evidence? Again, give reasons.

3 a) Read source D. How can you tell that Ilse's friend is frightened?
 b) How does this source help you to understand why the Nazis banned listening to the BBC?

THE JEWS

A How German Jews were restricted before the war.

One group of people was treated even worse than Poles or Russians. They were the Jews. In *Mein Kampf*, Hitler said that the people needed a single enemy. He chose the Jews. From the start, the Germans were encouraged to hate them.

The Nazis had made life difficult for German Jews long before the war. Some of the restrictions are shown above. In addition, the SS stopped customers going into Jewish shops. Jews who went out with non-Jewish girls were sent to concentration camps.

Life grew worse in November 1938, after a Jew shot dead a German official in Paris. The Nazis hit back: German Jews were fined; their children were not allowed to go to school. The SS organised two nights of violence against Jewish shops and synagogues. They called it 'Crystal Night' because so much glass was broken.

During the war, Jews living in occupied Europe faced the same hardships as those in Germany. And new laws were passed to make their lives even worse. These pictures show some of them.

Even Jewish rations were different: some foods, such as cherries and coffee, were forbidden to Jews. In the summer of 1941, a kindly visitor offered one Jewess some proper coffee. The old lady said 'No'. She was afraid that her neighbours would smell it and tell the police.

Hitler did not want Jews living in any country which he controlled. In Poland alone, there were 3 million of them. Some were used as slave labour. When they could no longer work, they were made to dig their own graves and then shot. The rest were rounded up and forced to live in ghettoes. This photograph shows the entrance to the ghetto in Lodsz, Poland. The sign warns of 'danger' of disease, forbidding entry on pain of death.

In the Soviet Union, the SS had special squads to kill Jews. Over 33,000 were machine-gunned at Babi Yar in just two days in September 1941. In November, the Nazis tried out a new idea. About 1200 prisoners in a concentration camp were gassed to death. It was an omen for the future.

B CURFEW FOR JEWS | WIRELESS SETS CONFISCATED | JEWS FORCED TO WEAR YELLOW STAR | JEWS NOT ALLOWED ON PUBLIC TRANSPORT | JEWISH RATIONS REDUCED

The Warsaw Ghetto

D A beggar in the Warsaw ghetto, summer 1941. In 1933, Goebbels had said it was 'stupid' to say that 'the Jew is a human being'.

E Jan Mawult lived in the Warsaw ghetto. He wrote in his diary:
The child of the ghetto has forgotten how to laugh. Its face is twisted into an adult snarl, marked by bitterness. Childhood has ceased to exist.

F Statistics of the Warsaw ghetto, set up in November 1940.
Population: 400,000-500,000
Total with jobs: 65,000
People per room: 9.2 on average
Warsaw rations (in calories per day): Jews 184; Poles 669; Germans 2613
By February 1943: only 70,000 were still alive. About 56,000 of these died after an uprising that month. They were shot, burned alive or sent to concentration camp.

G Liliana Zuker-Bujanowska lived in the Warsaw ghetto. In 1946, she wrote about it.
(Spring 1940) Every day new laws were announced. One of the worst was that all Jews ten years and older had to wear a white band with a blue Star of David on their left upper arm. After a few days they extended the law to all Jews. Even babies in carriages had to wear armbands. The penalty for not wearing them was concentration camp or death.

Then the hell started! The Germans made what they called 'raids for the bands'. They walked the streets with big rubber sticks and beat everyone they felt like, as long as they wore the white band. Now they were sure whom to hit. Gangs of youths ran the streets throwing stones through the windows of shops owned by Jews. The Germans picked young people from the streets and sent them to work camps in Germany.
(Winter 1940-41) Twice a day each person was given a bowl of watery soup and 300 grams of black bread. [The] houses were breeding places for typhoid and other diseases. People became so weak that they just lay down on the sidewalks and died of hunger and cold. There were corpses, sometimes covered with paper, other times half naked – someone had already stolen pieces of their clothing. There was no morgue. Most of these corpses were taken by the garbage men.

Every law has a number of consequences. Some may be economic; others may be political. The Jews suffered in various ways because of Nazi laws. Some consequences were more important than others.

1 a) Read page 50. List all the laws which the Nazis passed about Jews.
b) Write the letter P beside those which had political consequences.
c) Write the letter E beside those which could have had economic consequences. Explain how you chose these.
d) Which consequence do you think was most important for Jews? Please answer carefully.

2 Study this page.
a) How does source D help you to understand life in the ghetto?
b) How does source G help you to understand life in the ghetto?
c) Which do you think is more useful for this task? Explain your choice.

3 a) Read the caption to source D. How did the Nazis show that they did not think Jews were human?
b) How do you think the writer of source E might have replied to Goebbels?

Mussolini himself was rescued by the Germans in September 1943. He was put in charge of a new Fascist republic in northern Italy. The rest of Italy declared war on the Germans. And the Allies slowly advanced northwards.

Meanwhile, the Allies planned to attack Germany from the west. That meant that troops had to land in Normandy in occupied France. The plan was called Operation Overlord. It began before dawn on 6 June 1944. They called it D-Day – 'D' for 'Deliverance'.

That day, over 150,000 men waded ashore. Within a month, there were millions of them. Spies had actually told Hitler both the time and the place of the Allied invasion. But he did not believe their reports.

The Allied troops steadily pushed eastwards. In August 1944, Paris was liberated. By December, German troops were having to defend their own borders. The last year of the war was about to begin.

A The Allies advance on Germany.

In January 1943, the Allies asked the Germans to surrender unconditionally. Hitler refused. So the Allies had to keep fighting until they had beaten the German and Italian armies.

Throughout 1943, the Russians gradually pushed the Germans out of the Soviet Union. By January 1944, they had won back two-thirds of their land. That same month, the siege of Leningrad ended after 880 days; a million people had died.

The damage to the USSR had been huge. The Germans had wiped out whole villages; millions of Russians were actually living in holes in the ground. The USA and Britain had helped the USSR with tanks, planes and food. As Stalin later said, the British gave time and the Americans gave goods – but the Soviet Union gave human lives.

In 1943, Anglo-American troops in Africa crossed the Mediterranean. Their next main target was Italy. As they advanced, Mussolini was sacked and a new Italian government made peace. But it only controlled southern Italy; the Germans still controlled the north.

B In June 1944, Britain was attacked by a new weapon – the V1 pilotless flying bomb. The V2 (shown above) came next. It was a rocket bomb and killed over 2700 Britons.

An official Soviet history gave this version of the D-Day landings.

In June 1944 when it had become obvious that the Soviet Union was capable of defeating Hitler's Germany with her forces alone, England and the USA opened the Second Front.

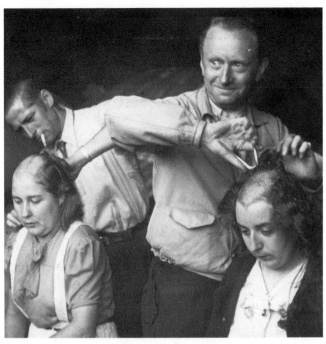

C US troops helped a colleague ashore in Normandy on 6 June 1944 after his landing craft had been hit.

D Anne Frank was a Jewish girl in hiding in Amsterdam. This was what she wrote in her diary on 6 June 1944.

'This is D-Day,' came the announcement over the British Radio and quite rightly, 'This is *the* day'. The invasion has begun! [It] still seems *too* wonderful, *too* much like a fairy-tale. Could we be granted victory this year, 1944?

I have the feeling that friends are approaching. We have been oppressed by those terrible Germans for so long that the thought of friends and delivery fills us with confidence!

E Elisabeth von Stahlenberg was German. Her husband, Hugo, was a Nazi. This is what she wrote in her diary on 6 June 1944.

Went out around midday – saw groups of people in the street. I thought there had been an accident, but it was far far worse. The English and Americans have invaded France.

Hugo and his friends talked until after midnight. They say it is the beginning of the end. The enemy have superiority on air, sea and land. What will happen? What will happen to us?

G Paris is liberated: these women are being punished for collaborating with the Germans.

Sources D, E and F show different attitudes to D-Day. The historian must work out why they differ and what we can learn from them.

1 Put these events in the order in which they happened:
   a) Paris was liberated.
   b) The siege of Leningrad ended.
   c) The D-Day landings.
   d) Mussolini was rescued by the Germans.

2 a) Read sources D, E and F. Write down one opinion from each source.
   b) How do sources D and E differ about the landings?
   c) Why do they differ? (You should think of at least two reasons.)
   d) Think hard. How do sources D and E give a different impression to source F?

3 a) Look at source G. What can you work out about people's feelings about these women?
   b) What do you think the women's feelings are? Give reasons.

DEATH OF THE DICTATORS

A   Berlin in February 1945.

By 1945, Hitler was a sick man. For years, his doctor had been giving him drugs – 92 different medicines in the last two years alone. At times, he no longer thought straight. In February 1945, he had at least one stroke.

The German generals knew they could not win the war. But Hitler was losing touch with reality and would not listen. Every day, he gave orders to his armies – whether they existed or not.

In April 1945, Russian and American soldiers met at Torgau on the River Elbe. Yet Hitler stayed confident: the stars predicted a German victory. Meanwhile, 90,000 teenagers and grandfathers prepared to defend Berlin.

The Soviet attack on the city began on 16 April. It was a bitter final battle. The Russian people had suffered so much at the hands of the Germans. Now, the Soviet soldiers could punish the people of Berlin for that suffering.

The war's atrocities were not yet over. Women were raped. The best that German troops could hope for was a beating; at worst, they were kicked to death. Meanwhile, Soviet tanks edged their way through the Berlin streets.

On 28 April, Mussolini and his mistress were shot by Italian   partisans   . Their bodies were strung up in front of a petrol station in Milan. This photograph shows their bodies.

Hitler planned to kill himself rather than suffer the same fate. First, he married his mistress, Eva Braun. Then, he dictated his will to his secretary. It said that he had never wanted a war: it was all the fault of the Jews.

On 30 April, he and his wife committed suicide. Their bodies were soaked in petrol and burned. On 1 May, Goebbels announced Hitler's death on the radio: he had died, said Goebbels, leading his troops. It was a hero's death.

Hitler had chosen Admiral Doenitz to take over from him. Doenitz said that the fight against communism must go on – but it was pointless. On 7 May, the Germans unconditionally surrendered. The war in Europe was over.

C   The red flag flying over the Reichstag: 2 May 1945.

D In 1945, German officer Heinz Landau was fighting on the outskirts of Berlin with his friend Wolfgang.

I saw a shell explode in the midst of my friends. All of them were either dead or terribly wounded. I found what I dreaded most – Wolfgang minus his legs. I grabbed hold of my last friend's head and yelled in agony, 'Wolfgang, Wolfgang!' He opened his eyes and smiled – then realised what had happened. His lips moved, but his voice was so weak in all that din. I bent close with my ear to his lips.

'Shoot me, Kamerad, for God's sake, shoot me.' His hand squeezed mine, then let go. A quick burst through the head, and Wolfgang was at peace.

E Ilse Koehn was a teenager, hiding from the Russians (1978). Her grandmother brings her news:

Everyone has survived. They threatened to shoot Grandfather a couple of times because he didn't have a watch. Vladimir saved him each time. He saved Hertha when they almost raped her. [Vladimir] is a young Russian lieutenant, who has taken a liking to pretty Lisa Gerber. He lives at the Gerbers' now. Thanks to him, we got away with no more than a black eye.

F So near to peace: this American machine-gunner was killed by a sniper's bullet on 5 May 1945.

1 Please answer in complete sentences.
a) Why did the Germans defend Berlin so fiercely?
b) Why did Hitler commit suicide?
c) Why do you think he wanted his corpse burned?
d) Why do you think Goebbels said that Hitler died a hero's death?

2 a) Which photograph would have most annoyed Hitler? Explain how you decided.
b) Think carefully. What sort of questions do photographs not answer?
c) Which source gives the best idea of what the war was like? Explain your answer carefully.

3 Devise two captions for source B. The first should be for a German newspaper. The second should be for an Italian newspaper.

4 Hitler blamed the war on the Jews. What do *you* think caused it? Please write a detailed answer.

THE HOLOCAUST

A Poland, 1942. A German soldier is about to shoot this man because he is Jewish.

Months before Hitler died, Allied armies had been making discoveries in occupied Europe. They had come across concentration camps. They were shocked by what they found. Even some Allied reporters thought it was just an Allied propaganda stunt.

The Nazis had set up concentration camps for their enemies in 1933. They were run by the SS; many junior staff were ex-convicts. The inmates included opponents of the Nazis, as well as gypsies, homosexuals and Jews. By 1939, there were six camps with 21,000 prisoners.

The more land the Germans took over, the more Jews there were to lock up. There were 3 million in Poland alone. In January 1942, the SS leaders decided on a new policy. They called it the 'Final Solution': they would kill all Jews.

New death camps were built. Gas chambers were installed in them because shooting would have taken too long. Jews from all over Europe were sent there in cattle trucks. Many thought they were going to labour camps. In fact, they were going to die. At Treblinka, the time from arrival to death could be as little as 30 minutes.

In 1943, 10,000 people a day died in the gas chambers of Auschwitz. Nothing was wasted: blood and ashes were turned into fertiliser; hair was made into cloth; gold was sent to the bank.

Not all the prisoners were gassed. At Dachau, some were used for 'medical research'. They were put in ice-cold water to see how long a human being could survive. At Belsen, people died of hunger or disease. Rats as big as rabbits ate the corpses which lay everywhere. Towards the end, food was so short that living prisoners ate dead ones.

Hanging, shooting, torture and over-work were all used to kill the Jews. There were about 8½ million Jews in occupied Europe in 1941; by April 1945, the Nazis had murdered about 5½ million.

The SS leader Heinrich Himmler said in 1943 that the killings were 'an unwritten page of glory in our history'. He tried to keep it unwritten. Before the war ended, orders went out to destroy the camps to keep them secret. But time ran out. The Allies decided that parts of some camps should be preserved – a permanent reminder of the war.

B British troops liberated Belsen; this girl survived . . .

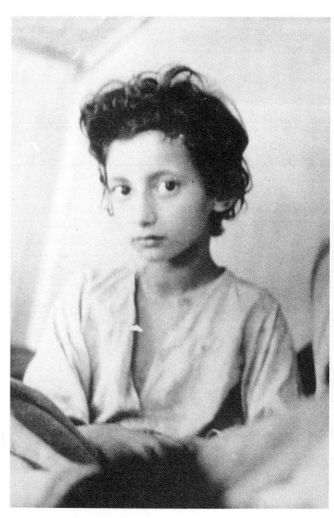

G British soldier James Palmer was sent to help clean up Belsen. This account was published in 1991.

On our left was a hay cart. It was full of dead, naked bodies, who all looked like children and babies. It was horrific, and the stench was wicked. Some of us vomited. The bodies were like skeletons with the bones showing clearly. The eyes had sunk into their sockets and their jaws were hanging loose. Bodies were lying around the huts and looked like bundles of rubbish.

H Heinrich Himmler said in 1943:

We shall never be rough and heartless when it is not necessary. We Germans are the only people in the world who have a decent attitude towards animals. [We] will also assume a decent attitude towards these human animals.

Every source is useful but some are more useful than others for a particular enquiry. It depends on what the historian is studying. The historian must also decide whether a source is reliable or not.

C . . . and those in the truck did not.

D Robert Bruckner was in Dachau camp from 1938-39.

Beside the huts was a grass strip, and next to that was an electric fence, and then a river and an SS camp. There were watchtowers outside the SS camp. The SS men in the watchtowers would play this little game. They threw a handkerchief down on the grass, and you weren't allowed to go on the grass. They told this man to fetch the handkerchief. If you said you couldn't fetch it they would shoot you. If you went on the grass to fetch it, the other man would shoot you from the watchtower.

E Dorothea Binz was head wardress at Ravensbruck. Lord Russell described her in *The Scourge of the Swastika* (1954).

One of Binz's favourite sports was to ride her bicycle into a group of women who were standing nearby. As they were so weak they were generally knocked down. She then rode over them, laughing as she did so. She also delighted in setting her dogs on the inmates. One day she set her dog on a Russian woman. One of the woman's arms was torn off.

1. Who or what were: (a) Heinrich Himmler; (b) the 'Final Solution' and (c) Auschwitz?
2. a) Read the written sources. What did Himmler promise?
   b) Do you think the Jews *were* treated decently? Give reasons.
   c) What can you learn from source G about how prisoners were treated?
   d) Which source do you think best illustrates Nazi attitudes towards the Jews? Explain how you decided.
3. Some people today claim that the death camps are a propaganda myth. Do these sources provide reliable evidence that this is wrong? Explain your answer.

| 250,000 | 600,000 | 600,000 | 731,000 | 1,380,000 | PROBABLY 2,500,000 |
| SOBIBOR | BELZEC | CHELMNO | TREBLINKA | MAIDANEK | AUSCHWITZ |

F Deaths in the Polish camps.

WAR IN THE FAR EAST

On 8 May 1945, victory in Europe was celebrated on VE-Day. But the Second World War was not yet over. Fighting was still going on in the Pacific between the Allies and the Japanese.

After the summer of 1942, the USA had been on the offensive. Their plan was to push the Japanese out of all the islands they had conquered. They began in August 1942 when they invaded Guadalcanal.

It took them six months to win back the island. And this was just the first of a series of long and bitter battles. The American plan was called 'island hopping'. One by one, they would capture each island before finally attacking Japan itself.

In October 1944, the US and Japanese navies fought the Battle of Leyte Gulf. It was the greatest naval battle in history – and the Americans won. The Japanese fleet was destroyed.

That same month, the Japanese came up with a new weapon: kamikaze pilots. They were trained to crash their planes onto American ships. They hoped that the explosives they carried would damage a ship. Japanese men queued up to become kamikaze pilots; it was seen as an honourable way to die.

U. S. ARMY OFFICIAL POSTER

We'll Finish the Job!

B An American poster of 1944.

The British, too, were fighting the Japanese. The Japanese army had captured Burma in 1942 and had even crossed the frontier into India. An Allied attack in 1942–43 had failed and it was 1944 before the Japanese were beaten at Imphal. It was the Japanese army's worst defeat on land.

The British Major-General Wingate successfully used guerilla tactics but it was a long, hard struggle. Captured Allied soldiers were badly treated in prisoner-of-war camps. Thousands were poorly fed and over-worked; some were tortured and beaten.

The Philippines fell in February 1945. By then, American troops knew what a bitter battle they had on their hands. American losses were huge. Japanese soldiers believed that it was a disgrace to surrender. So they fought to the death.

The closer the Americans got to Japan, the fiercer the land fighting grew. The two islands closest to Japan were Iwo Jima and Okinawa. About 4000 US troops died at Iwo Jima; another 12,000 were killed before Okinawa was captured.

The question going through American minds was: if it's like this on the islands, how many Americans will be killed if we invade Japan?

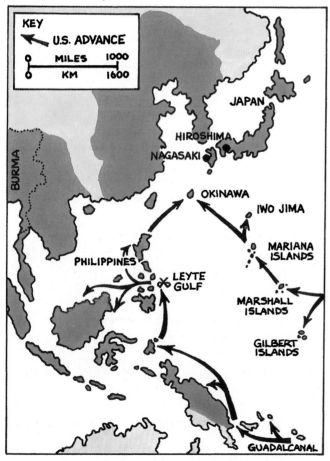

KEY

← U.S. ADVANCE

MILES 1000

KM 1600

JAPAN
HIROSHIMA
NAGASAKI
BURMA
OKINAWA
IWO JIMA
MARIANA ISLANDS
PHILIPPINES
LEYTE GULF
MARSHALL ISLANDS
GILBERT ISLANDS
GUADALCANAL

A The war in the Pacific. Areas occupied by Japan are shown in orange.

Kamikaze pilots

C Ryugi Nagatsuka was a kamikaze pilot. Bad weather forced him and his leader to return to base in 1945. He described his commanding officer's reactions in *I was a Kamikaze* (1972).

The C.O. [was] trying to keep a check on his rage. '[Your comrades] were ready for death before they took off. You funked it. You have dishonoured our squadron and I am ashamed of you. Why didn't you die like heroes?'

His whole body shook with anger. 'Shame on you!' [he] shouted. 'It is as if you had deserted in the face of the enemy. I am putting you under arrest. You will copy out the sacred words of the Emperor until further orders!'

D The same writer described a successful kamikaze attack in October 1944 (1972).

Lieutenant Seki crashed into the carrier, exactly between the flight deck and the hull. The bomb he was carrying exploded, making a huge hole in the side of the ship. Another Zero followed Seki and, with [great] skill, plunged into the hole already ripped open in the ship's side. Another Zero crashed into a second carrier and set it on fire . . . The heroes of this first suicide mission had undoubtedly kept their eyes wide open right up to the fatal moment of the crash.

E A photograph taken in October 1944, just after a kamikaze attacked this US ship.

F Japanese kamikaze pilots. When the war ended, over 4600 had died; another 5000 were ready to die.

G A song sung by kamikaze pilots before take-off.

After the battle, our corpses will be strewn
On the green mountain slopes,
Our corpses will rest at the bottom of the sea.
We shall give our lives for His Majesty,
We shall die without regrets.

1 a) Study source B. Which Americans do you think this poster was aimed at? Explain how you decided.
   b) What message was it trying to get over?

2 a) Read sources C and G. How can you tell that kamikaze pilots were expected to die?
   b) How useful is source C for understanding Japanese attitudes towards the war? Explain your answer.
   c) Study sources C and D carefully. How reliable do you think these sources are for understanding kamikaze attacks? Give reasons.

3 a) Which of all these sources is propaganda? Explain how you know.
   b) What can a historian learn from the source you have chosen?

THE ATOM BOMB

KUNIO YAMASHITA
山下國男
14 DEC 1946

A Hiroshima after the explosion (August 1945). The inset picture shows a survivor with severe radiation burns.

American and British scientists had spent most of the war developing an atomic bomb. President Roosevelt had known about it from the start but, in April 1945, he died. Harry Truman took over as president. So it became his job to decide what to do with the bomb.

On 16 July 1945, the scientists exploded one in the New Mexico desert. It was a success. Even while the countdown was going on, the parts of another atomic bomb were being taken across the United States. Their destination was Japan.

On 26 July, the Allies sent the Japanese an ultimatum. It told them to surrender without conditions or there would be 'prompt and utter destruction'. The message did not mention the atomic bomb.

The Japanese did not give in. So, on 6 August, an American plane took off for the Japanese city of Hiroshima. It carried one atomic bomb. The Americans had chosen Hiroshima because it was a major port and an army headquarters.

The bomb exploded at 7.16 am. A massive ball of fire erupted; for a few seconds, the temperature in the centre of the city reached 6000°C. Within minutes, a mushroom of cloud had grown 8 miles (15km) high. Inside it were millions of pieces of wood, metal, glass – and people. Over a mile away, trains and cars were blasted into the air.

On 9 August, the Americans dropped a second bomb on the city of Nagasaki. It had the same effects. Five days later, the Japanese told their forces to stop fighting. On 2 September, Japan officially surrendered. The Second World War was over.

But the war was not over for the people of Hiroshima or Nagasaki. About 70,000 people died when the bomb was dropped on Hiroshima. At the centre of the explosion, people were simply vapourised . Further away, they were badly burned.

But, within days, a new kind of death had appeared. Survivors developed fever and burns. Others found their hair falling out; their gums bled; parts of their skin just rotted away. No one knew what was happening. Today, we know these illnesses were caused by radiation.

Why was the bomb dropped?

B S L Case: *The Second World War* (1976).
Truman knew that by using the [the bomb] he could probably bring the war to a speedy conclusion. He decided that, to save American lives, he was justified in using this new and most terrible of all weapons.

C *Postwar World* (1975).
It was well known to Truman, long before the test, that the Japanese [wanted] peace. There were several actions Truman could have taken which would have brought the war to a swift conclusion. He could have started by warning the Japanese of the new bomb; he could have encouraged the Russians to declare war weeks earlier; he could have [told the Japanese that they could keep their Emperor]. Truman knew all these roads to peace, but he did not take any of them.

D *The Sunday Times* (1991).
The popular view [in Japan] is that the Americans dropped atomic bombs on the Japanese rather than on the Germans for racial reasons.

E Vadim Nekrasov (a Soviet writer): *The Roots of European Security* (1984).
Officially [the USA] claimed that the bombings were aimed at bringing the end of the war nearer and avoiding unnecessary bloodshed. But they had different objectives. The bombings [were to frighten] other countries, above all the Soviet Union.

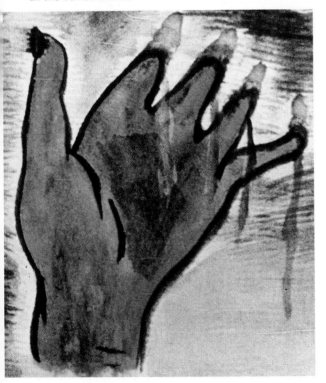

F Akiko Takakura painted this in 1975. He remembered a corpse with 'fingers burning with blue flames. The fingers were shortened to one-third and distorted'.

36,000	NAGASAKI (A-BOMB) 1945
62,000	BRITISH CIVILIANS (GERMAN ATTACKS) 1939–45
70,000	HIROSHIMA (A-BOMB) 1945
83,000	TOKYO (U.S. FIRE-RAID) MARCH 1945
approx.**100,000**	DRESDEN (G.B. AIR RAID) FEB. 1945

G Approximate figures, comparing deaths from the atom bombs with other attacks in the war.

Why was the bomb dropped? This is the sort of question which historians try to answer. As you can see, they do not agree about the causes.

1. a) Why was the bomb dropped, according to source B?
   b) How do sources C, D and E disagree with source B?
   c) Which source casts doubts on source B? Explain your answer.
   d) Suggest reasons for the views given in sources D and E.
   e) Does that mean these views are unreliable? Explain your answer.

2. a) What do you think was the most likely reason why the bomb was dropped? Explain how you decided.
   b) Do you think the atom bomb brought progress? Explain your answer.

I have got some stumps in my field that I should like to blow out. Have you got any atomic bombs the right size for the job?

After Hiroshima, some people still did not understand the bomb. This letter was sent by an American farmer in October 1945.

WAR CRIMES TRIALS

1920   1930   1940   1950   1960   1970

A The courtroom at Nuremberg; the defendants sat in a long dock, listening through headphones. Goering is on the far left of the front row.

In 1919, Germany was judged guilty of starting the First World War. Yet the German leaders were never put on trial. The Kaiser himself fled to Holland where he lived until his death in 1941.

After the Second World War, it was different. Leading Nazis were put on trial at Nuremberg in November 1945. Many people did not want a trial: they thought that important Nazis should just be shot. Even Churchill drew up a list of top Nazis who should be shot. Stalin went further; he wanted 50,000 German officers put to death.

Hitler, Goebbels and Himmler had committed suicide. But 21 leading Nazis went on trial, including Goering. They were accused of waging the war and various war crimes.

Hundreds of witnesses gave evidence. Some told of being tortured in concentration camps; others spoke of being forced to work in Germany. During the trial, a film of the concentration camps was shown. One defendant said afterwards,

'When I see such things I am ashamed to be a German. It was those dirty SS swine!'

The prisoners were quick to blame each other. The generals claimed that they had just been following orders. But one person was willing to accept responsibility. Hermann Goering, boss of the Luftwaffe, said, 'I personally gave the orders to bomb Warsaw, Rotterdam and Coventry.'

The trial lasted until October 1946. Three of the 21 were acquitted; seven were sent to prison; the other 11 were sentenced to death. They included Goering but he cheated the executioner by taking a cyanide capsule just hours before he was due to hang.

The Nuremberg trials were just the first. Others followed. In all, over 300,000 German soldiers and Nazis were tried by the Allies for war crimes. Nor did it end at Nuremberg. As late as 1987, ex-Gestapo Chief Klaus Barbie was sentenced to life imprisonment for war crimes in France.

Some other Germans and Japanese were luckier. Japanese army doctors who experimented on prisoners-of-war went free. The Americans did a deal with them: the doctors told the United States about their research into germ warfare.

What the accused said

B Dr Hans Münch was an SS pathologist at a centre near Auschwitz. Forty Auschwitz doctors were tried in 1947; only Münch was acquitted.

In June 1944, the camp commandant ordered him to take his turn for the selection routine which decided which new prisoners would go to the gas chambers.

Münch said no.

'Nothing was going to make me do it,' he told Austrian TV. 'I travelled to Berlin and told my chief that [it] was against my principles. He said that certainly I didn't have to.'

He added, 'I don't think anyone in the SS was forced to do what they did against their will.'

C Adolf Eichmann was Gestapo chief responsible for the Jews. He was hanged in 1962. At his trial, he said:

I do not consider myself guilty legally. I merely received and carried out orders.

D Franz Stangl, a camp commandant, was sentenced to life imprisonment. In 1971, he recalled first finding out about the gassings.

Michel (a nurse) and I agreed that what they were doing was a crime. We considered deserting. But how? Where could we go? What about our families?

E 'Guilty!' says this German poster after the Nuremberg trials.

F This American cartoon of 1945 looked forward to the Nuremberg trials.

Immediately after the war, people had very strong feelings about what had happened. They were especially shocked by the 'Final Solution'. So it is not surprising that many people were biased against all German soldiers. This affected what they wrote – and what they drew.

1 a) Who was put on trial at Nuremberg?
b) Why do you think the Allies were keen to try them?
c) What happened to the defendants?

2 a) Study source F. Whose skulls do you think you can see? Explain how you decided.
b) What did the artist think of the Nazis? Give reasons.
c) Suggest reasons why this cartoon is biased.
d) Does that mean that it has no value for a historian? Explain your answer.

3 a) Read sources B, C and D. Which people thought the killings were wrong?
b) Which source do you think gives the best idea of why Germans were willing to kill Jews? Explain your choice.
c) Do you think what Eichmann said was a good defence? Explain your answer carefully.

RUDOLF HESS

Seven men were sent to prison as a result of the Nuremberg Trials. One of them was Rudolf Hess. He had been Hitler's deputy when war started. He was sentenced to life imprisonment.

For over 50 years, historians have argued about the Hess case. Even now, we cannot be certain. The British have secret files on him which will not be made public until 2017. These two pages present some of the evidence about the case.

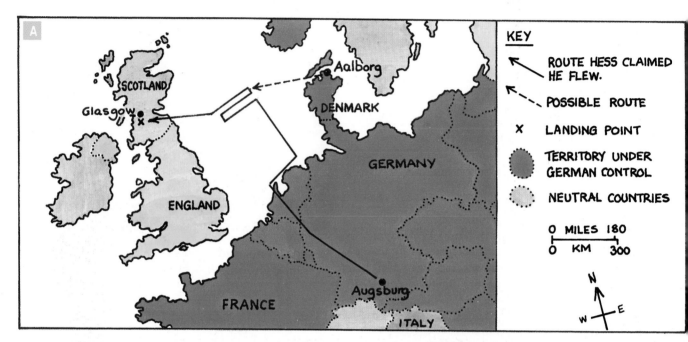

KEY

↖ ROUTE HESS CLAIMED HE FLEW.

↖ POSSIBLE ROUTE

✗ LANDING POINT

TERRITORY UNDER GERMAN CONTROL

NEUTRAL COUNTRIES

On 10 May 1941, a single German Messerschmitt 110D crashed in Scotland. The pilot parachuted to safety. At first, he claimed to be Alfred Horn and said he had an important message for the Duke of Hamilton.

The next day, he met the Duke and said he was really Rudolf Hess, Hitler's deputy. At first, the Duke did not recognise him. Hess said that Hitler did not want to fight England. So he had come on a peace mission. Historians cannot agree about whether Hitler knew of Hess's plan.

At first, Churchill was suspicious and kept the news secret. But German radio reported that Hess was missing. It added that he was suffering from a mental disorder.

Hess claimed he had flown from Augsburg in Germany – a distance of 1260 miles (2020km). His route is shown on the map. But this was beyond the range of this plane. Some people have suggested that the plane was fitted with special fuel tanks.

In any case, if Hess set off at 5.45 pm, he should have reached the British coast at about 9.15 pm, if he had flown directly. In fact, the recorded time was 10.15 pm. And he flew in from the east; according to his own version, he should have arrived from the south-east.

Those are not the only puzzles. If you look at the map, you will see that Hess wasted an hour zig-zagging over the North Sea. Why would he want to do this?

The plane is a problem, too. The fuselage markings on the wreckage were NJ+OQ. Planes with this marking were based in the Baltic Sea. Their main base was Aalborg in Denmark.

On the evening of 10 May, Goering phoned the commander of fighter squadrons on the Dutch coast, telling him to scramble all aircraft. The orders were to shoot down Hess's plane.

To add to the problems, Hess's adjutant claimed he took this photograph of Hess taking off from Augsburg. The plane has no extra fuel tanks. All of this has led some people to wonder: was the pilot really Rudolf Hess – or a double?

In 1990, the Soviet Union released wartime secret papers about Hess. In one of them, a Czech spy said why he thought Hess had flown to Britain (adapted).

The common view that Hess had flown to Britain all of a sudden is not true. Hess had been corresponding with the Duke of Hamilton. All the details of the flight were discussed.

However, Lord Hamilton did not write letters to Hess himself. All Hess's letters to Lord Hamilton went to the British secret service. They wrote the letters to Hess from 'Lord Hamilton'.

E The Duke of Hamilton's son replied:
They clearly got it wrong. There is no evidence that M16 was writing to Hess to get him to come over. On 3 May 1941, the secret service wrote to my father saying that plans to do that had been put [off]. Days later, Hess arrived in the country.

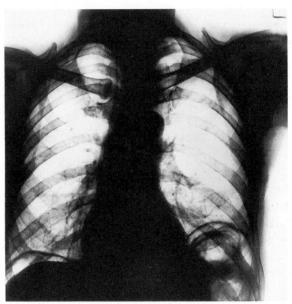

F The 1973 X-ray of Hess's chest.

C Hitler with Hess, before the war.

Hess spent the rest of the war as a prisoner in Britain. He wrote to his wife via Switzerland. She believed the letters were from her husband. In 1946, he was sentenced to life imprisonment in Spandau Jail in West Berlin. One by one, the other Nazi prisoners were released. After 1966, Hess was left in Spandau Jail alone.

In 1973, he was given a full medical examination by a British doctor, Dr Thomas. Hess was X-rayed. One X-ray showed no scars on his chest. This was odd because Hess had been shot in 1917 and his lung had been wounded. Yet there was no trace of this wound in 1973.

Hess was returned to Spandau Jail. Guard duties were shared between Britain, France, the United States and the Soviet Union. The USA, Britain and France suggested that he should be freed. The Soviet Union always refused.

Hess refused to see his wife and son for 23 years. When he did have visitors, guards were always present. He was never allowed to talk about the flight to Scotland. Anything he wrote was destroyed. In 1987, aged 93, Rudolf Hess committed suicide.

Sometimes we think we know the truth about the past but we later find out we were wrong. Is this the case with Rudolf Hess?

1 a) What evidence is there to suggest that the man in jail *was* Rudolf Hess?
  b) What evidence is there to suggest that he wasn't?

2 Most people thought that the prisoner *was* Hess. If this is true, how could you explain:
  a) how the plane reached Scotland?
  b) why the marking fitted a plane based elsewhere?
  c) the zigzag over the North Sea?
  d) the lack of chest scars?

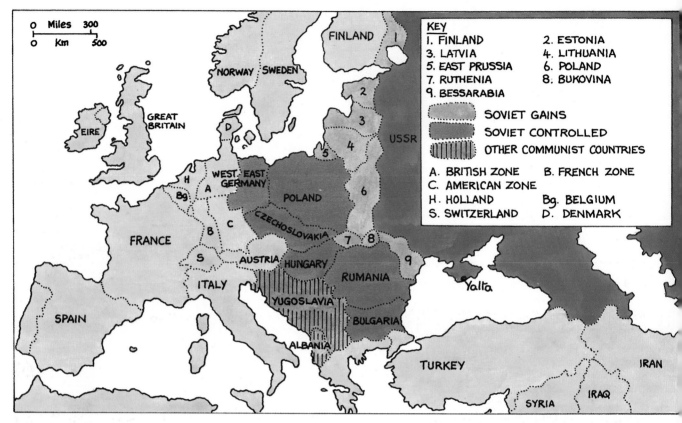

A Europe after the war.

By February 1945, it was clear that Germany would be beaten. So Roosevelt, Stalin and Churchill met at Yalta to decide what should happen after the war. Their main problem was what to do with lands they had captured from Germany.

First, there was Germany itself. The Allies agreed that Germany would be divided into four zones. Each would be occupied by one of the winning Allies: the USA, Soviet Union, France or Britain. Berlin, the capital, would also be split.

The Red Army had entered Poland in March 1944. Stalin did not intend to give up the Polish land he had gained by his agreement with Hitler. So the new boundary remained. In return, Poland was given German land to the west.

The Allies also agreed that each liberated country could choose whatever kind of government it wished. But Roosevelt and Churchill knew that eastern countries would have no choice. The Soviet Union was in a powerful position; its army already controlled most of eastern Europe. Stalin intended that these countries would become communist.

In April, President Roosevelt died. When the Allies met again at Potsdam in July, President Truman represented the USA. Half-way through the conference, there was a general election in Britain and Churchill's party was beaten. The new Prime Minister, Clement Attlee, took over from him during the conference.

There was much that the leaders disagreed about. Stalin wanted Germany to pay reparations; the others did not. In the end, Stalin had his way. Factory machines were stripped from the Russian zones of Germany and Austria and taken back to the Soviet Union. Equipment was taken from the other zones, too. Germans in the east were pushed into forced labour – just as the Russians had been in the war.

In eastern Europe, a 'People's Democracy' was set up in each country which Stalin controlled. Soviet advisers moved in. All anti-communists went to a labour camp or were killed.

Stalin was creating a buffer zone to protect the Soviet Union. He was determined that it would never again be attacked from the west. By March 1948, all of eastern Europe was firmly under communist control.

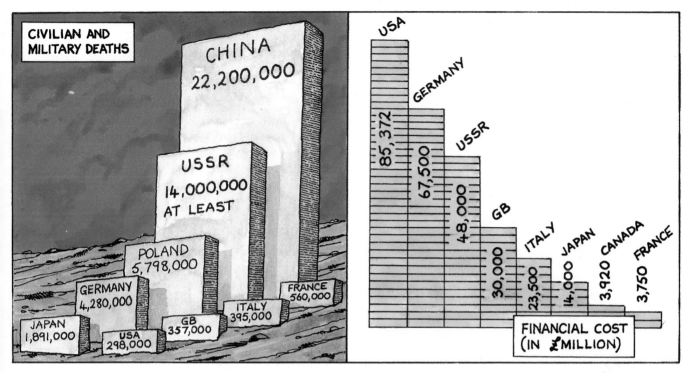

CIVILIAN AND MILITARY DEATHS

CHINA 22,200,000

USSR 14,000,000 AT LEAST

POLAND 5,798,000

GERMANY 4,280,000

FRANCE 560,000

ITALY 395,000

GB 357,000

JAPAN 1,891,000

USA 298,000

USA 85,372

GERMANY 67,500

USSR 48,000

GB 30,000

ITALY 23,500

JAPAN 14,000

CANADA 3,920

FRANCE 3,750

FINANCIAL COST (IN £ MILLION)

C The cost of the war. The larger casualty figures are approximate and the financial figures are estimates based on 1946 currency.

B Churchill, Roosevelt and Stalin meeting at Yalta. The Allied leaders were nicknamed 'the Big Three'.

" MY GOODNESS, MY HAPPINESS ! "

D A cartoonist's views of the Yalta meeting.

1 a) Compare sources B and D. Who are the three people on the left in source D? Please list them in order.
b) Who do the sealions stand for?
c) What message was the cartoonist trying to give?

2 a) What happened to Germany after the war? (There is more than one consequence.)
b) Write down at least one economic consequence for Germany.

c) Write down one political consequence.
d) What consequences did the war have for the Allies?
e) What kinds of consequences were these?

3 a) Study source C. Who do you think suffered most as a result of the war? Explain your answer.
b) Study source A. Who do you think suffered most as a result of the war? Explain your answer.
c) Explain why your answers are the same or different.

... AND A NEW WORLD CLUB

A The Allies began calling themselves the 'United Nations' in 1942.

At Yalta, 'the Big Three' agreed that the League of Nations must be replaced by something better. The world needed a new organisation, with real powers to keep the peace.

From April to June 1945, representatives of 50 nations met at San Francisco. They signed a charter to set up this new organisation; it would be called The United Nations. This UN Charter said the UN's aims were:

- to avoid war
- to encourage nations to co-operate
- to promote better standards of life
- to ensure everyone gained basic human rights

The major nations were anxious that the United Nations should succeed, where the League of Nations had failed. The League of Nations had used sanctions to stop countries fighting; they had not worked. So it was agreed that the United Nations should have an army.

It would not be its own army. Whenever it needed troops, member countries would send some of theirs. Sometimes they would be posted between the enemy sides; at other times, soldiers would work as observers.

The United Nations has a *Security Council* which meets if there is an emergency. Ten of its members are elected for just two years; the others are permanent members. These are the Soviet Union, USA, Britain, France and China.

The League of Nations had been weak because some countries had not joined. All the major powers of 1945 have a key role in the United Nations. They can ask other countries to use sanctions to stop fighting – or they can send in a UN peace-keeping force.

Each of these five countries has a veto. In other words, if they do not agree with a policy, they can block it. The veto was not intended to be used often. But the USA and the Soviet Union often used their veto during the first 40 years.

Once a year, the UN's *General Assembly* meets. Every member of the UN can send representatives along; every country, big or small, has just one vote. In 1993, there were 180 members.

There is one other change from the old League. The UN has a Secretary-General; he is a respected politician from a smaller country. The success of the UN partly depends on how good the Secretary-General is.

B In 1948, the UN agreed on a Universal Declaration of Human Rights. These were its key points.

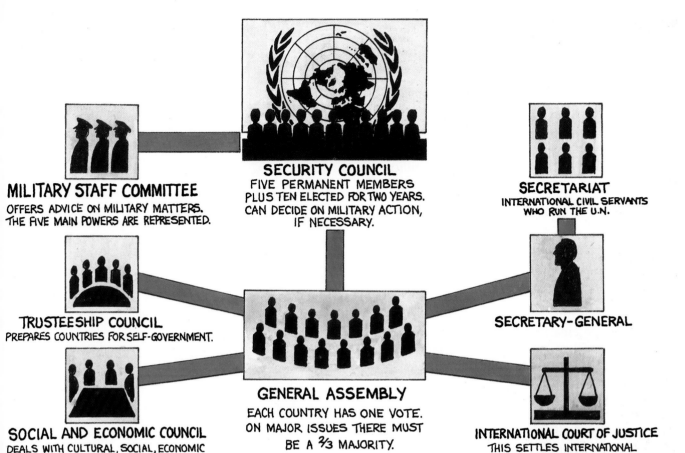

MILITARY STAFF COMMITTEE
OFFERS ADVICE ON MILITARY MATTERS.
THE FIVE MAIN POWERS ARE REPRESENTED.

SECURITY COUNCIL
FIVE PERMANENT MEMBERS
PLUS TEN ELECTED FOR TWO YEARS.
CAN DECIDE ON MILITARY ACTION,
IF NECESSARY.

SECRETARIAT
INTERNATIONAL CIVIL SERVANTS
WHO RUN THE U.N.

TRUSTEESHIP COUNCIL
PREPARES COUNTRIES FOR SELF-GOVERNMENT.

SECRETARY-GENERAL

SOCIAL AND ECONOMIC COUNCIL
DEALS WITH CULTURAL, SOCIAL, ECONOMIC
AND HEALTH MATTERS.

GENERAL ASSEMBLY
EACH COUNTRY HAS ONE VOTE.
ON MAJOR ISSUES THERE MUST
BE A ⅔ MAJORITY.

INTERNATIONAL COURT OF JUSTICE
THIS SETTLES INTERNATIONAL
DISPUTES.

C How the United Nations is organised.

There is often more than one version of something that happened in the past. When this happens, historians must compare them to decide which is more reliable. The one they use may affect how they interpret the event.

D Emery Kelen attended the meeting at San Francisco. He recalled this story in *Peace in Their Time* (1963).

A story too good to be new, was [repeated] in San Francisco [about] Wellington Koo, [a Chinese representative]. At a banquet, they say, he was seated next to a senator who did not trouble himself much with his neighbour; but from time to time, he would turn to him and inquire: 'Likee soupee?' or 'Likee meatee?'

When the time came for speeches, Dr Koo addressed the gathering in [excellent] English. After sitting down, he turned to the senator and asked, 'Likee speechee?'

E *Postwar World*, a magazine, told the story like this (1975).

An amusing story about Wellington Koo was recorded by Emery Kelen. During one banquet the ambassador was placed next to an American senator who did not pay him much attention except for asking: 'Likee soupee?' and 'Likee meatee?' After dinner Dr Koo rose and made a speech in perfect English. After sitting down he turned to the senator and casually inquired: 'Likee speechee?'

1 a) How is the United Nations different from the League of Nations?
   b) Why were these changes made?

2 a) Read sources D and E. Which one was written first?
   b) How do the two accounts differ? (There's more than one answer.)
   c) Does source D say this event happened? Quote from the source in your answer.
   d) Does source E say the story is true? Explain your answer carefully.
   e) Which do you think is the more reliable account? Please answer carefully.

3 a) Copy out the diagram (source C).
   b) Underline in red the parts of the UN which are concerned with keeping the peace.
   c) Underline in blue the parts which are directly concerned with helping people. Explain your choices.

THE REFUGEES

| 1920 | 1930 | 1940 | 1950 | 1960 | 1970 |

The UN's aim was to keep the peace in the future. But the people of Europe had more urgent problems. By 1945, there were about 20 million people without a home. Whole families were walking the streets; everything they owned was tied up in a bundle or pulled on a cart.

Some of these refugees had left their homes to avoid the fighting; others had left to avoid being persecuted by the Nazis; a third group was leaving lands being taken over by the Communists.

But many simply didn't have a home any more. Across Europe, nearly 3 million homes had been destroyed; another 3 million had been damaged. And that did not count damage done in the USSR and in Germany itself.

The UN had its own organisation to deal with the problem. It had been started in 1943, even before the UN itself was founded. Over the next six years, it spent about £600 million on helping refugees; most of the money came from the USA.

B A German refugee family with their remaining possessions (1945).

The UN took over old barracks and POW (prisoner-of-war) camps to house the refugees. Many wanted to start new lives overseas. Most Jewish refugees were just too frightened to go back to their homes. Some went to settle in Israel when it was founded in 1948.

Most countries limited the number of refugees they would accept. In general, they did not want old or sick people. Many families had to choose between staying in a camp as a family – or starting a new life overseas, leaving a sick grandparent behind on their own.

Perhaps Russian refugees suffered more than most. There were up to 7 million of them. Over 50,000 had fought for Germany. They knew what would happen to them when they were returned to the Soviet Union; many committed suicide before they could be killed.

But even genuine Russian POWs or slave labourers suffered. Over a million of them were executed or ended up in Soviet labour camps. Stalin did not trust people who returned from the west. He thought that POWs were traitors because they had surrendered. On the side of one trainload of refugees was written: TRAITORS TO THE HOMELAND. Even many Nazi war criminals were treated better.

A This Polish girl's home no longer exists; she portrays it as a scribble.

C James Palmer was a British soldier stationed in Germany after the war (1990).

Thousands of Polish and Russian prisoners and [refugees] were in camps, [waiting to go home]. The Poles and Russians hated each other's guts. There were armed conflicts between the two camps.

To add to the confusion, the Poles and Russians each formed vengeance squads to go out and destroy local German farms and communities. The situation was so bad that British troops had to guard isolated farms from the Poles and Russians.

D In 1945, Elfriede Grabowski was a German teenager when Russian troops overran her home town (1990).

One of my sisters was shot dead in front of us all. We were all raped, my mother included. All the German population, plus all 'foreigners', Poles etc. were rounded up and housed in cellars in burnt-out houses. Most of us were put to work rebuilding our own houses so that Russian families could be moved in.

[She was later taken to work in the Soviet Union but escaped back across the border.]

We were put in a camp, a transit camp. It was fine there. We had pillows, blankets, food, clothes – there was a cupboard there, toothpaste, a toothbrush! My God, hadn't seen one for years, or soap. We got packets from the Red Cross. I always give something to the Red Cross, when people are collecting. No more lice. I was free.

When studying causes, remember that there may be more than one cause of an event. The same goes for consequences. The changes that take place are not always an improvement for everybody.

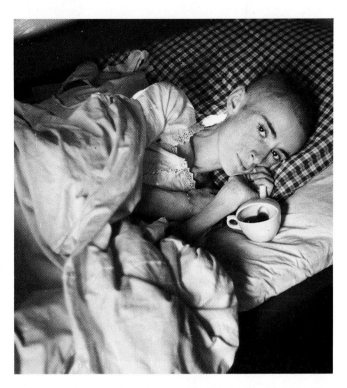

F She, too, had no home. This young girl was recovering in hospital after being found at Belsen concentration camp.

E People wandering through the remains of Berlin in 1945.

Remember that an event may have more than one cause and consequence.

1 This question is about causes.
   a) Why were there so many refugees in Europe in 1945?
   b) Why did many Jewish refugees choose to go to Israel?
   c) Why do you think many countries did not want to take in old or sick refugees?
   d) Why did Stalin kill some Russian POWs?

2 This question is about consequences.
   a) What consequences did the war have for:
   (i) the girl in source A; (ii) the people in source B and (iii) the teenager in source D?
   b) Which of these consequences was the most serious? Explain with care.

3 a) Study *all* the sources. For which people did the end of the war bring progress? In each case, explain why.
   b) For which people did the end of the war not bring progress? Again, explain why.

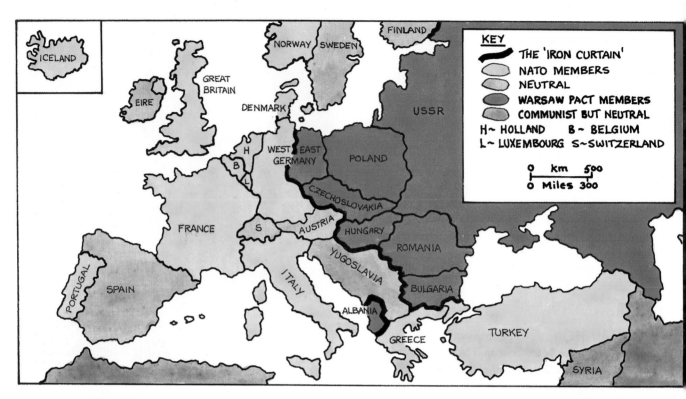

A East versus west. How Europe divided in the years after the war.

'The Big Three' met for the last time at Potsdam in July and August 1945 but already the Allies did not trust each other. The Americans did not warn Stalin before they dropped the atom bomb on Hiroshima. He thought that the USA might turn on the Soviet Union, now that the war was over.

The US President, Harry Truman, did not trust Stalin, either. He wanted to stop the spread of communism. He was worried, too, about what might happen once the Soviet Union had produced its own atomic bomb.

After Japan surrendered, the British Prime Minister, Clement Attlee, said, 'Peace has come once again to the world.' But a new kind of war was just beginning. They called it the Cold War. It was not fought with guns but with words. Yet it still frightened people. Above all, they feared a nuclear war.

In 1946, Churchill gave a speech in the USA. He told Americans that 'an iron curtain has descended across the Continent': on one side were the free countries of western Europe; on the other were communist countries controlled by Stalin.

Of course, there was no curtain – but there *were* minefields to stop people fleeing to the west. There *were* barbed-wire fences guarded by soldiers ready to shoot anyone trying to escape. And, in 1961, the Communists even built a wall in Berlin to keep their citizens in.

The USA and Britain could only watch as eastern Europe turned communist. But, in 1947, President Truman took action when it looked as though this might happen in Greece. The Greeks were given American aid and the Communists were defeated. The USA promised to help any country which was threatened by communism. The policy was called the Truman Doctrine.

Truman believed that poor people were most likely to support communism. So, in 1947, the USA launched the Marshall Plan. It offered $17,000 million to help European countries. Britain got the most – over $3000 million. Stalin thought it was a capitalist plot, so eastern Europe turned down the offer.

In 1949, the western nations joined together in NATO (North Atlantic Treaty Organisation). It was a military alliance to defend western Europe. The USSR said it threatened them. So, in 1955, they formed their own organisation – the Warsaw Pact. It was just ten years since the war; already, Europe was divided into two armed camps again.

B President Truman's view . . .

The Russians were not in earnest about peace. They are planning world conquest.

C . . . and Stalin's view.

Perhaps you think that, because we are allies of the English, we have forgotten who they are and who Churchill is. They find nothing sweeter than to trick their allies. And Churchill? Churchill is the kind who will slip a [coin] out of your pocket, if you don't watch him.

D The USSR President, speaking in 1945.

We cannot forget that our country remains the one socialist state in the world. Victory does not mean that all dangers to our state have disappeared.

E Attlee, the British Prime Minister, gave his views about the USSR in *A Prime Minister Remembers* (1960).

The Russians had shown themselves even more difficult than anyone expected. After Potsdam one couldn't be very hopeful any longer. It was quite obvious they were going to be troublesome. The war had left them holding positions far into Europe, much too far. I had no doubt they intended to use them.

This war is the greatest step on the way to Bolshevist *world revolution!*

STALIN

G German wartime leaflet dropped on British troops. (Bolshevist means Communist.)

There were many causes of the Cold War. It was not just caused by what politicians did; it was also caused by what they said.

1 What was (a) the iron curtain, (b) the Truman Doctrine, (c) the Marshall Plan, (d) NATO and (e) the Warsaw Pact?

2 a) What did source G warn was going to happen?
   b) Look at source A. Was source G correct? Please answer carefully.
   c) Why do you think this leaflet was dropped on British troops?

3 a) What can you learn about Allied attitudes from sources B and E?
   b) What can you learn about Russian attitudes from sources C and D?
   c) Do you think the Cold War was inevitable? Please answer in detail.

4 a) How reliable is source F? Explain your answer.
   b) What can a historian learn from source F? (There's more than one answer.)

F These postage stamps showed the Soviet Union as a friend.

THE BRITISH LEGACY

Britain had won the war but she was a loser, just as much as Germany was – only people did not realise it. The war had cost Britain dearly. She had been forced to sell £1000 million of foreign investments. Meanwhile, she had piled up new foreign debts worth £5000 million.

By 1945, Britain had bigger debts than any other country. On top of that, Britain borrowed £1100 millions from the USA, to be paid off over 50 years. The last payment would be due in 2001.

At the time, few realised what these problems meant for the future. The urgent task was to repay the debts. The only way that Britain could do this was to earn money by exports. So the best goods were not on sale at home.

Rationing was even tighter than during the war and lasted until 1954. At one point, even bread was rationed. Princess Elizabeth had to save up 100 clothing coupons for her wedding dress.

Churchill had led the country to victory. But, in the 1945 general election, the electors voted for a change. The Labour Party won the election, with a huge majority.

A 1945 SHOPPING EXPEDITION

I'M SORRY, MADAM. WE'VE SOLD OUT OF LADIES' SHOES, GLUCOSE, CHOCOLATE CREAM BISCUITS AND BICYCLE BELLS.

AND STRAW SCHOOL HATS ARE BANNED ANYWAY!

NO GRAPEFRUITS, CHILDREN'S SANDALS OR Nº 8 BATTERIES AVAILABLE

A Everything was in short supply in 1945. You could not even buy a bucket and spade at the seaside. None had been made for five years.

"But, darling, I just <u>had</u> to buy it, it was such a bargain."

B This 1947 postcard joked about the sale of wartime equipment. In fact, many planes from the Battle of Britain were sold to Spain.

During the war, the government had published the Beveridge Report. It had recommended unemployment pay, family allowances and a proper health service. The Labour government now had the chance to introduce all these reforms. In 1948, the National Health Service (NHS) began offering free medicines and treatment.

At first, there was full employment as British industry set out on its export drive. But other countries, too, were busy exporting. French and Italian production was growing at twice the rate of production in Great Britain. And our share of world trade was dropping.

British industry was using out-of-date machinery and technology. The ship-building industry had plenty of work during the war. But American shipyards were more efficient. And German industry had to rebuild itself; its factories and equipment would be new.

There was one other great change. Men from the colonies had fought alongside the British in the war. They saw no reason why Britain should go on ruling their countries. They wanted to be free and the Labour Party agreed with them. The process began in 1947 when India became independent. Forty years later, the British Empire no longer existed.

C The year is 1963. Dutch people place flowers on the graves of British servicemen. Over 55,000 British and Commonwealth bomber crews had died. These men had had the technical skills which Britain needed after the war.

D Lieutenant-Colonel Goodson was in Germany after the war. He described what he saw in *The Last of the Knights* (1990).

In Cologne, I saw a man pushing a broken-down baby carriage from the rubble. [He was] picking up bits of steel and iron. He was one of the big steel [manufacturers], who had been a multi-millionaire. The scrap he was collecting was to help rebuild his factory.

I [visited] Hingeley, an English friend who was trying to rebuild the Dunlop tyre factory, which had been flattened by the bombing. They had got a patched-up boiler going in the snow. Out in the open, some hundred men were straining to feed simple tyre-building machines.

'You see those men over there in the rubble?' Hingeley asked. 'They are from the second shift, putting in extra time, helped by their wives and children.'

I supposed he was paying them overtime. He laughed.

'We don't pay them at all! We can't invest any money. But after two months' work, we give every worker a bicycle tyre. That's worth a fortune on the black market.'

I flew back to England, where I found the tyre factories were on strike.

E Almost one house in three had been damaged. These ready-made prefabs were one solution.

1 a) What political change happened in Britain after the war?
  b) What changes did the Labour Party introduce?
  c) Why were goods still rationed after the war?

2 a) List all the consequences of the war you can find.
  b) Which of these were long-time consequences? Explain how you know.
  c) Which of the consequences do you think was most serious for Britain? Give reasons for your choice.

THE WAR'S LONG SHADOWS

"Coca-Cola is a registered trade mark of The Coca-Cola Company."

A Where the American troops went, so did Coca-Cola. The war helped it to become a worldwide drink.

The war's consequences are with us still. In western Europe, the main countries desperately wanted to avoid another war. Churchill had said, 'We must build a kind of United States of Europe.'

In 1957, six nations set up the European Economic Community. At first, Britain stayed out – but she then spent over a decade trying to get in. It was 1973 before she became a member.

Roosevelt said that American troops would leave Europe within two years of the end of the war. He was wrong. In 1993, US troops were still stationed in Europe. Meanwhile, the USA and the Soviet Union eyed each other suspiciously in a Cold War which lasted until the 1980s. In 1950, US troops began fighting in Korea to hold back the Communists; from 1965 to 1973 more GIs fought in Vietnam for the same reason.

The war had turned the USA into the world's economic super-power. Marshall Plan funds helped countries such as West Germany and Austria to recover. By 1960, West Germany had become the richest country in Europe.

The USA also helped recovery in Japan. American money helped to rebuild shattered Japanese industry. Japanese businessmen copied American styles and the country soon had the world's fastest-growing economy.

The Soviet Union's grip over eastern Europe lasted long after Stalin's death in 1953. There were attempts to break free in Hungary (1956) and Czechoslovakia (1968) but the Soviet Union kept its control. It was 1989 before the communist empire began to fall apart.

Fifty years afterwards, the war continued to cast shadows over many people's lives. In the 1990s, it was discovered that, for over 40 years, medical schools in West Germany had used specimens taken from people murdered by Nazis. Meanwhile, the survivors of Auschwitz and other camps could not forget; many still suffered nightmares.

In Japan, they have tried to forget. School history books are censored; some of its history has been rewritten. In 1991, a Japanese television crew interviewed people in the street about an event which had happened 50 years earlier – Pearl Harbor.

Many teenagers had not even heard about it. Some were astonished that Japan had actually fought the USA. One of them asked the TV crew a question:

'Who won?'

B The 1942 film *Casablanca* set out to persuade Americans that they needed to be involved in world affairs. It has remained a popular film.

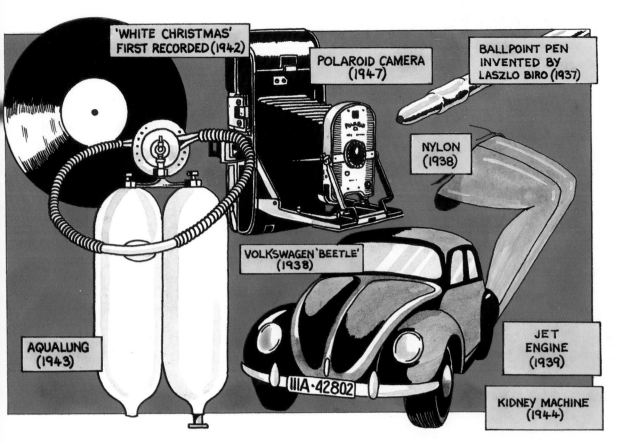

'WHITE CHRISTMAS' FIRST RECORDED (1942)

POLAROID CAMERA (1947)

BALLPOINT PEN INVENTED BY LASZLO BIRO (1937)

NYLON (1938)

VOLKSWAGEN 'BEETLE' (1938)

AQUALUNG (1943)

JET ENGINE (1939)

KIDNEY MACHINE (1944)

IIIA·42802

C Some of the more lasting products of the war years.

Looking back in 1991

D Hans Teske was a German paratrooper in the war. His homeland was taken over by Poland and became communist.

I can't return to my home. I can't ever meet my family or schoolfriends in my hometown. The ones who are still alive were all expelled. It is as if I died in 1945.

I accept that major war crimes were committed in the name of Germany. But my family and friends were the victims of major atrocities by the other side. We are now 50 years on, but we still hear little of the crimes committed by the Russians, Americans and the British.

E John Hall was an RAF pilot.

England was a lovely place to be in those days, with country towns almost bare of traffic, and friendly people whose beliefs were the same as yours. I did appreciate what a good place England was to fight for. I still often think of four good friends, who were killed, and I still miss them.

F Sidney Lawrence was a POW in Japan and survived the Nagasaki bomb.

I wouldn't have missed the whole experience of the war. People today haven't a clue what it is like to endure this kind of suffering. It will do one of two things to you. It will either make you bitter and full of hate or it will be the making of you.

Every time August comes around, I am aware of the strange [uneasiness] that affects all of us who survived the bomb. I try to ignore it, but I begin to feel very strange.

1 a) Read page 76. Write down all the consequences of the war that you can find.
 b) Decide if each change was political, economic or social. Write P, E or S beside each answer to (a).
 c) Read sources D, E and F. What long-term consequences did the war have for each of these men?

2 Look at source A. The war boosted the availability of Coca-Cola worldwide. Does this mean that the war brought progress? Explain your answer carefully.

3 You need to watch a short extract from *Casablanca* to answer this question.
 a) What evidence of propaganda can you see?
 b) The film is fiction. Does that mean that it is useless as a historical source? Explain your decision.

A Jill and Dusty were still hard at work near Windsor after the war.

It had been a good war for British farmers. An extra 7 million acres of land were producing food by 1945. There had been record harvests and new technology had been introduced. By 1945, four times as many tractors were being used as before the war.

The British people entered peacetime healthier than ever before. Despite the shortages, people had actually had a better diet, with more protein. Fewer mothers died in childbirth during the war than before it.

Women's lives had changed in other ways, too. Younger women had been conscripted and many had gained freedoms which were unthinkable in the 1930s.

After the war, many stayed at work: there was a labour shortage. But, when the men returned, many women were thrown out of better-paid jobs to make way for them. Often, they ended up in low-paid factory and office work.

For Japanese women, there was a bigger change. They got the vote for the first time. They were still ruled by their emperor, Hirohito, but even his position had changed.

Until 1945, the Japanese people had looked upon him as a god. In August 1945, he had spoken on radio to tell his people that the war was over. It was the first time that ordinary Japanese had heard his voice. Soon afterwards, he lost most of his powers and became a figurehead ruler.

There was change, too, in the Soviet Union, although not the sort that many wanted. Millions of Russians hoped that victory would mean more freedom at home. They were disappointed: Stalin's rule was as harsh as ever.

Marx had said that everyone would be equal in a communist country. But people found that the gap between ordinary people and Communist Party officials had grown. Their standards of living were getting further apart.

After 1940, Soviet secondary school pupils had to pay fees and these continued after the war. The children of communist officials were getting a much better education than poor children. It was a far cry from what Russians had expected when they had their revolution in 1917.

B The House of Commons was bombed in 1941. MPs moved to the House of Lords to continue their debates.

C In June 1944, the SS killed 642 men, women and children in the French village of Oradour. The village has been preserved as the Germans left it. The postcard shows it as it was before the war.

The Second World War was over but new wars were just beginning. On the day the Japanese surrendered, a communist called Ho Chi Minh declared independence for Vietnam. Fighting went on there for most of the next 30 years.

Millions of other people did not live to enjoy peacetime. One of them was a young Jewish girl called Anne Frank. She had spent much of the war hiding from the Nazis. In August 1944, they caught up with her. She died at Belsen in March 1945 just a month before it was liberated.

She did not survive but her diary did. In July 1944, there had been an attempt to kill Hitler. 'Now I am getting really hopeful,' she wrote, 'now things are going well at last.' Throughout the war, people had kept hoping that better times were coming; the year 1946 found the survivors still hopeful for the future.

D Anne Frank was remembered on this Dutch stamp of 1980.

---

1 a) Write down all the changes which took place between 1939 and 1945.
b) What stayed the same?
c) Why is it hard to say what the most important change was?
d) Were the changes all for the better? Explain your decision.

2 a) Look at source C. How is the village different today from what it was in 1939?
b) How can you tell that the postcard shows the same place?

3 Look back through this book. You may choose any one picture to sum up the effects of the war. Write down your choice and explain why you chose it.

GLOSSARY

adjutant – officer who assists the commanding officer

Aryan – according to the Nazis, the superior race; it included Germans

atrocity – very cruel or brutal act

ATS – Auxiliary Territorial Service

Bolshevik – Russian communist

civilian – someone not in the armed forces

collaborating – working with the enemy

concentration camp – prison camp where the Nazis held their enemies

conscientious objector – person who believes it is wrong to fight

conscripted – made to join the forces

convoy – merchant ships, escorted by Royal Navy ships

demilitarised – without troops or weapons

democracy – country in which everyone may vote

dictator – person with total power

fall – autumn

Fascists – supporters of Mussolini, named after the Fasces, their symbol

Führer – Leader

ghettoes – separate areas where Jews were made to live

GIs – American troops; 'GI' (meaning General Issue) was stamped on their equipment

incendiaries – bombs causing fires

kamikaze – suicide pilot (it means *divine wind*)

liberated – freed

Luftwaffe – German air force

militia – army of citizens, trained for war

mobilised – got ready for war

nationality – group of people forming a nation

neutral – not supporting either side

pacifism – belief that it is wrong to fight

partisans – people who fought behind enemy lines

pathologist – doctor who carries out post-mortems

patriotic – loving one's own country

persecuted – treated badly and repeatedly harmed

pillaging – robbing

plebiscite – vote by all adults on a special question

proletariat – poor working class

rationing – allowing a limited amount of food

reparations – payments in compensation for damage

republic – country without a king or queen

sniper – soldier who picks off individual opponents by rifle-fire

Soviet Union – see USSR

SS – armed branch of the Nazi Party (short for *Schutzstaffeln*)

traitors – people who betray their country

U-boat – German submarine (from *unterseeboot*)

ultimatum – final demand, including a threat of what will happen if it is not met

USSR – name given to Russia after the revolution (short for *Union of Soviet Socialist Republics*)

vapourised – turned into gas

WAAF – Women's Auxiliary Air Force

Zero – Japanese fighter plane